Authenticat

a Country Dwelling

by Judy Condon & Sherry D. Pees

Library of Congress Cataloging-in-Publications Data
Authenticating a Country Dwelling by Judy Condon & Sherry D. Pees
ISBN 978-0-9912026-3-8

Oceanic Graphic Printing, Inc.
105 Main Street
Hackensack, NJ 07601

Printed in China

Layout and Design by Pat Lucas,
lucasketch_design@yahoo.com
pat-lucas.fineartamerica.com
Edited by Trent Michaels

Table of Contents

About the Authors

Judy Condon retired her position as Superintendent of Schools in two districts in Connecticut when her husband Jeff was transferred to Virginia in 2002. Between her administrative position in the school systems and owning Marsh Homestead Antiques, an antique shop in Litchfield, Connecticut, Judy soon discovered her move to Virginia left her with a great deal of time on her hands. Jeff suggested she consider writing the book she had always wanted to write, *Country on a Shoestring*; a pictorial and inspirational book for country decorators who wanted to achieve the 'look' on a limited budget. Judy wrote from experience as she and Jeff had owned a Litchfield, Connecticut home built in 1764 and each time Judy was ready to take on a decorating project, some other major catastrophe needed to be addressed. As a result, Judy created ways to achieve the country decorated home that she wanted at a fraction of the cost. Once the first book was published, readers asked "When is the next book coming out?" That was eight years and 28 books ago. Judy created the first 'house tour' book on the market in 2005 and has developed a following of dedicated readers one of whom remarked "I'd rather have a root canal than wait for your next book!"

Judy continues to write what has become known as 'the simply country' book series and is currently working on four books for 2015 but last summer deviated briefly from the series to write *Nothing Tastes as Good as Skinny*, a tough-love approach and Program for weight loss and weight loss management. As the subtitle indicates, 'this ain't no diet book'! Awareness for the book has been made with a number of editorials in national magazines and Judy has created a 'cyber support' group on Facebook. The website for the book is *www.asgoodasskinny.com*

Authenticating a Country Dwelling is a departure from the format of the 'simply country' series in that it is not a house tour book as her others are but an educational tool for learning about 18th and 19thC life through the use of photographs of homes. Judy has long felt that a pictorial book of country decorated homes was much needed and could demonstrate the two mind-sets and differences between authenticating and decorating a country home. After meeting and sharing ideas with Sherry D. Pees, an historian and period Home Consultant, Judy realized that the co-authoring of a book was the perfect venue for combining Sherry's expertise, knowledge and writing talent with Judy's experience as a photographer and writer.

Judy and Jeff returned to New England in 2009 and live in an early 19thC home in Douglas, Massachusetts which was shown in a previous book, *Back Home – Simply Country*. Judy enjoys spending time with her five children and seven grandchildren; particularly building memories at their family summer home in Maine. Judy and Jeff, both avid readers, still manage to find time to play golf and travel.

Judy maintains a website *www.marshhomesteadantiques.com* and may be reached at the toll free number 877-381-6682 or via email at *marshhomestead @gmail.com*. Judy's books are sold in over 200 country shops, on her website and through ebay® and Amazon®.

Sherry D. Pees, a native of Ohio, has spent most of her adult life studying, teaching and consulting with clients who wish to create a home that represents that of the 1780-1850's era. Sherry grew up on a farm, the eldest of three children and as such the first to be sent to the barn and fields at an early age to help out. Married to Ken Pees for fifty years, they and two sons operate a soybean and corn farm known as Pees Poor Ridge Farm in Northwest Ohio. Their sons are the 8th generation of German farmers since 1730 who carry the surname..

Sherry graduated from Ohio Northern University where she majored in history and completed a four year degree within three years. Returning to Ada, Ohio as a newly hired high school teacher in the same school from which she had graduated three years previously, caused some confusion. It was a challenge for Sherry as a first year teacher to assert herself in the role of authority with many students who had known her for years only as Sherry.

After two years of marriage and the birth of their first child, Sherry and Ken decided that Sherry would remain at home to raise their children. Having enjoyed the art of teaching, Sherry elected to teach evening Adult Education classes at two satellite locations of Ohio State University on the topic of creating a period home. During the first half of each semester, Sherry used slides to convey what has now become known as 'Pees Points'. The second half of the semester involved the touring of authentic period homes and museums in the area. Sherry modestly attributes the popularity of her classes to the latter half of the curriculum. However, the fact that many of her students have hired her over the years as a consultant in creating the type of period home she introduced in class, is an endorsement of her knowledge and interest she generates on the subject. As the demand for Sherry's expertise became more in demand, the natural career path was to become a period Home Consultant.

Sherry has worked with a number of families in Washington, Massachusetts, Ohio and Texas. Sherry has served as President of the Hardin County Sesqui-Centennial Celebration. Sherry has also served as consultant for the 1840's non-profit restoration of the McKinnis Farmstead near Findlay, Ohio and the Swiss Haus and Garten Project near Bluffton, Ohio.

When not consulting or helping on the farm, Sherry enjoys gardening and spending time with her three children and two grandchildren.

Sherry maintains a blog at *peespoorridgefarm.blogspot.com* and has written numerous articles for country magazines and publications. *Authenticating a Country Dwelling* is Sherry's first book.

Sherry is available for consulting with homeowners interested in creating an early dwelling place. Her seminar lectures about improving period and country style homes are educational and interesting. Sherry may be reached by email at *peesfarm@centurylink.net* or by phone at 419-759-2661.

Introduction

After filming hundreds of homes for the 'simply country' series, I've noted that while many of us country collectors strive to achieve the style of a 19thC home, the tendency is often to place our treasures in full display for our appreciation without careful attention to whether or not it is an appropriate placement.

There is a great difference between the home of a country decorator and the home of an authenticator. I am a decorator who is at fault for placing my finds in clear view with reckless abandonment as to what the original use of the treasure may have been. I look to mix textures and colors; sometimes old and new. In no way is this intended to be an apology however nor should any of the homeowners whose pictures are included in this book feel a need to justify how they have decorated their homes. The intent of *Authenticating a Country Dwelling* is as an educational perspective on history; a learning tool for those readers who wish to authenticate or replicate the homes of our early ancestors.

In all my years of filming homes for my series of country decorating books, I have found no one who is an authenticator to the extent of Joy Henson of Ohio. You may recall her home which I featured in *Welcome Home – Simply Country*. When Sherry D. Pees and I first discussed the concept of a book on authenticating, Joy Henson immediately came to mind and a revisit to her home was a necessity – not to mention the pleasure in seeing her again.

Joy Henson exemplifies what it requires to be an authenticator. She has a counter part – Lovey Makepeace for whom Joy has created not only a 'life' but a history. In Joy's mind, Lovey Makepeace was married to a young soldier who fought in the American Revolution under a Colonial Wainwright. At the war's end, Lovey and her husband Justice moved to upstate New York where for two years they tried to make a living farming the land. The cold, the rocky soil and the failure of producing successful crops were the motivating factors in accepting an offer from Colonial Wainwright to accept 40 acres of his land in an area known as the Western Reserve and which would eventually become Ohio. Lovey and her husband packed their belongings into a wagon and traveled for weeks over terrain that often required Lovey to walk rather than ride as the pathways were strewn with stumps and rocks. Lovey related during my initial visit that Mr. Makepeace at one point raised his shotgun to kill game for their dinner and the firing of the musket scared the horses and overturned the wagon scattering "Lovey's fripperry" for what seemed like a half mile.

Her history continued. At long last, they arrived and Mr. Makepeace began immediately to build a modest house for them with the help of Hiram Goodfellow, their hired man. Not long after the completion of the cabin, Lovey related the day that changed her life. Mr. Makepeace and Goodfellow were off hunting rabbits when Mr. Makepeace tripped over a fallen log, his musket misfired and he was fatally wounded.

Now suddenly a widow, Lovey considered her options. She wasn't strong enough to endure a return trip to upstate New York and was appalled at the idea of being a burden on her family. Because her cabin was located along a route of great western expansion and travel by settlers, Lovey decided she could sustain a living by operating a tavern. Further, having experienced a trip west, she understand fully the importance of providing necessities for the women who were traveling with their families – sewing materials for mending clothes, a ladies parlor where concerns and fears could be shared. The creation of Lovey and Justice Makepeace has been the impetus behind the home which Joy and John Henson have created.

Joy Hensen exemplifies the difference between a decorator who can create a home which feels right to a 21stC inhabitant, and an authenticator who creates a home through imagination and fantasy which feels right to a 19thC homeowner. As Joy shared with me, "Lovey Makepeace dictates what goes in our home and how a piece is displayed. If it doesn't 'feel' right to Lovey, it doesn't belong".

Not everyone will embrace authenticating their country dwelling one hundred percent certainly and each of us may 'buy into' the effort and imagination at different levels. *Authenticating a Country Dwelling* is a pictorial and instructional tool with an historic base from which the reader may glean what is palatable and ignore that which is not.

Chapter 1

The Bed Chamber

When an authenticator uses appropriate textiles in a room, that space becomes more believable. In the 18th and early 19th centuries, textiles were the most expensive and treasured goods of a household – so valuable they were listed in probated wills and passed to the next generation as inheritance. The work endured to produce a linen bed sheet was worth as much as a cow. A center seamed linen bed sheet is a 'treasure' rightfully and proudly displayed on a rope bed rather than in a cupboard. An authenticator will be sure to turn the bed covering back to show that distinctive hand sewn seam. Here the owner has a checked homespun bolster with tape ties which later would be placed at the head of the bed, and an indigo checked bed covering. A blanket chest is rightfully at the foot of the bedstead and a clothes chest is nearby storing handmade clothing. The tied back curtains are simple and adjustable for those nights of lightning bolts or bright moonlight.

Textiles, appropriately added to a room, bring truth to the space. If your home is pre Civil War and striving for authentication is a goal, textiles should be hand hemmed. It makes a difference and adds credibility.

Every room needs an eye-catcher and here it is – the high bracketed shelf in a bedroom.

Originally, it would have provided storage for a rolled blanket tied with two strips of homespun cloth, a pair of period shoes, a stash of cases – the period word for pillow cases, and perhaps a lady's best bonnet. At present, its purpose is unfulfilled except for one lonely basket. An authenticator might consider adding some of those items listed above to 'age' the room to its furnishings. The eye notices the chair rail and follows it around the room. The bare window is period correct. Remember, not every house window, especially upper story ones, in the 18th and early 19thC needed "coverings"– a period term for curtains.

The portrait above the bed is one possible wall piece the early housewife would have hung on a bedroom wall. An embroidered sampler, a penned family genealogical record or a printed maxim could have been other options.

Whenever you think a room lacks appeal, no matter what accessories you have added, look up because the upper walls and ceiling are calling for attention.

Serious authenticators study how the early family lived. We can pretend this bedchamber is of a "middling" family with at least one adult who could read and write as evidenced by the quill and inkwell on the bedside table. The unmatched tester bed cloths are the best this early family could afford. Bartering allowed their child's portrait to be painted by an itinerant limner who traveled the countryside painting portraits and decorating interiors of homes with wall murals and stenciling.

Note that a candle burns more slowly when shielded from drafts.

We can imagine geese are being raised on this farmstead for meat and feathers as the large square pillow is firmly stuffed with feathers. It is an odd size which is a good thing as its shape was determined by fabric and stuffing available in the household at the time of its making.

The wall cupboard came welcomed, we can believe, from the wife's family at marriage. The only giveaway that this is a 21stC scene is the mattress because no feather tick lays this flat.

When you wish to authenticate the bedroom in your home, give your best attention to the bed. Every attempt should be made to conceal the appearance of a modern day mattress and modern standard size pillows. Place a goose down comforter under the bed covering and arrange it high and rumpled in the middle and over the mattress edge to soften the outer edges of the modern mattress.

Even better, pull the bed covering, the period term for bedspread, over the head pillows rather than tucking the covering under and over the pillows as is done today.

As collectors, many of us are drawn to early rocking horses and wish to display them in a prominent spot in our homes. However, here's a story about "the juxtaposed rocking horse".

A homeowner was attracted to a rocking horse and bought it at auction. It was destined for a child's room and raised to a blanket chest as folk art to be admired. The simple placement of a rocking horse can distinguish the difference between a decorator and an authenticator. A decorator will place the rocking horse wherever it pleases that person's eye. The authenticator would desire the rocking horse to be on the floor appearing as if ready for riding.

While both decorators and authenticators enjoy staging their homes, the mindset is different and produces different results.

Some country decorators and period authenticators view magazine and book photos inch by inch, even with a magnifying glass. In this view, some people first admire the old red mule chest. However, a few years later, the room will be recalled as the room with the sloped rafter wall. When building new home construction, incorporate memorable features like a sloped rafter wall, winder staircase, a ceiling loft, or a secret opening in the fireplace wall. Consider a low door in the knee wall, a high corner shelf in a rural bedroom large enough to hold a small leather trunk or install a bedside shelf.

Whatever room object our eyes find interesting at the moment is of little importance. What matters more is what element can be recalled a year later about the room. Interestingly, what is usually recalled is something structural.

Note the large square pillow on this rural bed. Certainly the 19thC homeowner owning this bed chamber kept a flock of geese for feather stuffing of bed pillows. Pillow size and shape were determined by the family's stock of saved feathers and fabric. Hence, pillows were odd sized and shaped.

The spool bed was produced by manufacturers using various woods; hence these beds were always stained dark walnut or mahogany to hide the different woods used.

The curved corners of this bed defines it as being made circa 1850 or later.

Spool beds and spool turned furniture when first introduced were made with screws instead of dovetails or a mortise and tenon joint. Spool beds were the first to use wood slats for supporting a bed tick. Previously, a rope web supported a bed's tick on a rope bed.

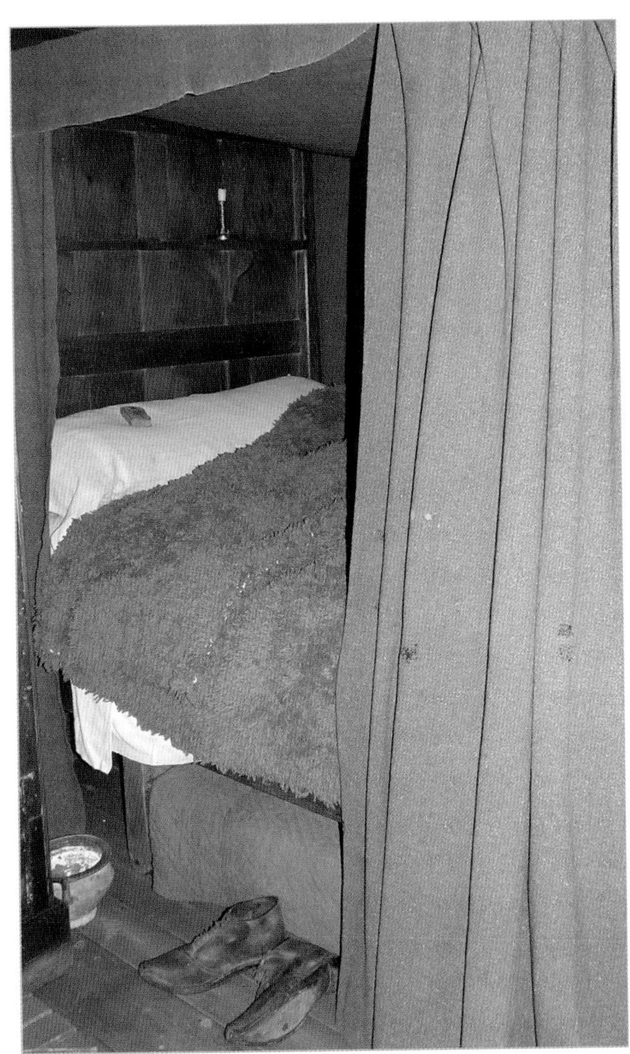

This homeowner has appropriately authenticated a mid 19thC bedroom as the portrait above the bed, the candle lighting device and the framed sampler are all period accessories showing that the homeowner has certainly done some homework. However, a lap desk on the bed would have caused great stress to the 1850's housewife as fear of ink stains or fire from a tipped-over candle would have been first and foremost in her mind.

Rather, an authenticator might place a period garment on the bed and a pair of early shoes on the floor.

This bedroom has the beginning of an authenticated space but the bedding textiles however hinder.

Changing out the red coverlet for the indigo one already on the bed is more true to the early 1800s. While the red coverlet is attractive to country decorators, authenticators know this red color was not available as a natural dye in this era. Replacing the cases for natural linen or windowpane indigo checked ones would add more truth to this early 19thC scenario.

The bedcover appears quite long and modern. Bed coverings seldom hung lower than the bottom of the side rail for several reasons. The underneath area was used for trunk storage which frequently had to be opened. Also mice were always unwanted visitors in early homes. They can jump and climb onto cloths.

The authenticator will follow history by portraying a bedroom as if an early family occupied it.

What a joy ! A sparse bed chamber. This period homeowner has done their homework and we authenticators appreciate the effort. If the reader is a novice authenticator, scrutinize this scene with a critical eye and learn. Note the following objects.

The bedstead is a tall four poster. Its canopy and side curtains could be hand woven linen. Bed steps exist for a needy housewife of small stature. An 'easy chair', referred to as a wing chair today, is a luxury for the husband, an elderly family member or visitor. Yes, a visitor when long ago bedrooms did receive visitors.

Window coverings, a period term for curtains, are of simple one-panel construction. Surely these are hand sewn with narrow 1/8 to 1/4 inch hems. Having only one top casing, the window coverings are hung on cord, string or woven tape. Windows are open because airing the bedchamber and bedding was important. To the far left is a high chest of drawers. It stores personal clothing and treasured bed linens. An additional feather tick has been aired and placed across the bed. What we call today the mattress was referred to as the bed ticks in the 18th and 19thC.

Because the room is so well appointed we can almost forget the electric crockery base lamp to the left. A better lighting device could be an electrified candle-like fixture carefully chosen.

Clearly work spaces in any room are a good idea. For example, placed on the floor near the ladderback rocking chair, a basket with knitting supplies and a knitted tippet will give clues to the housewife's proficiency. A bright window nearby brings good daylight for this work.

This wonderful bedchamber and its fireplace certainly conjure up all kinds of images for the authenticator. We can imagine a hired boy removing ashes from the firebox and laying in wood for warmth on the coming night; an orphaned niece repairing or remaking the bed and gasping upon finding a torn place in the linen sheeting. But where is the bed warmer?

Most of the activity of 21stC family life takes place on the home's first floor but in the past centuries, the staircase was busy with traffic going to and fro. In the upper chambers, in addition to bedrooms, there may have been a loom room, a wool room where picked wool was sorted and stored in piles on the floor, a hired girl's room, or a spinning room. The staircase traffic lasted all day until bedtime.

A hired girl's chamber is a good fit for "empty nest" period homeowners. To the fun group of authenticators, do take possession of the smallest empty room upstairs and re-stage it into a primitive, sparse space for a fictitious hired girl. Two of my clients in Texas did just that and named their fictional characters, "Phoebe" and "Hannah", creating an awesome chamber with an enclosed curtained bed, wide plank floor, a deer skin rug, wooden shoes, a few homespun garments and evidence of sewing and spinning skills. What fun!!! This upper room photo here has the same potential.

Let's re-stage it. First, the bedstead is too expensive for a hired girl because many a girl slept on a straw floor pallet, but the head of this 'pretend household' will allow Lisbet the use of it and the small table. Lisbet will carry her meals to her room and eat them there. She will do the following work: clean house, help with monthly washings, help prepare all meals, weed the garden, mend and sew, tease wool and spin it, and feed and care for foul.

The modern mattress is much too thick, so a straw tick with a corn husk tick on top will suffice. The bedstead's roping appears tight. The bedding is old but serviceable enough. We'll remove all evidence of electricity, artwork, rag and hooked rugs and curtains. Lisbet's trunk can remain under the bedstead. An old stool from the wood shed is ample enough seating for Lisbet. The room will be the best she has ever occupied and she feels fortunate to be hired by this family.

Oh what would an 18th or 19thC housewife have given to have a beautiful bedroom such as this? In fact, many contemporary decorators would be envious of this room.

An authenticator would look at it differently.

Rural bedrooms, like this one, were in past centuries "fitted out" as income allowed. To own a four poster bedstead signified that the early family or their ancestors had funds enough to own it.

This contemporary decorator is obviously attentive to detail as the bed covering is smooth and perfectly placed. In contrast, the 18th or 19thC female would have pulled the bed covering up and over the bolster and pillows.

This decorator has softened the room with the long textiles at the window. The spinner and weaver in a period farm family would have seen these present day curtains as a waste of yardage.

The beautiful chandelier to the 21stC home decorator adds an element of elegance to this lovely bedroom. In the 18th and 19thC, this ceiling light would have been too extravagant for this simple bedroom.

In the period bed chamber, a handmade rug would have been a necessity in cold winter. However because it would have been handmade, it would have been much smaller in size than that which the 21stC housewife could afford. The period housewife would find an area floor rug as pictured here well beyond their means, money-wise.

For centuries, terms describing what we today call the "bed" were this: Our ancestor's 'bedstead' is our bed frame while their 'bed' – usually a straw tick or sack of feathers or corn husks, wool pickings or bran – is our mattress. Their 'bed covering' is our bed spread and their 'bedding' is our bedsheets and blankets. Their 'cases' are our pillowcases. These old terms were commonly listed in old estate inventories and can be confusing to the present generation. It's fun to use these old terms. Furthermore, believe it or not, voicing these terms places the mindset in a past century which is a great asset when authenticating. Talking the talk reinforces the walk we make toward authenticating. Use the language of yesterday and you will soon see that ideas and answers about the early household come like magic to you.

There's an authenticator at work here. Here's why.

First, the room has a wide plank floor; its cracks between boards are narrow; hence the lumber was seasoned slow and sure. The low bed is a trundle bed for one or more sleeping children who need to be near parents. The indigo and white checked bed covering could have been hand woven by family or purchased from a local weaver if funds allowed.

The adult bedstead's headboard is against the knee wall of the second story. Its red pigment finish over maple cost a little more than average but the wife so wanted it. It is held together by four bed bolts, each about seven inches long, and a rope interlaced web. The bed covering is a woven coverlet loomed by an area weaver to whom the family took its spun and dyed wool yarn. The weaver could have supplied the linen warp for a price or barter. The coverlet needs to be pulled up and over the striped bolster and pillows and should not be tucked under the pillows as done today.

The framed piece above this bed could be a completed stitched sampler or a calligraphic maxim. In this era, bedroom exhibited wall items held personal value and were not decorative accessories. Authenticators could display one or more of these wall accessories; an old family marriage license, a family genealogical record, ancestral portraits or perhaps a church confirmation document.

The candlestand reserves the candlestick that lit the staircase for the night time climb to the upper story. It will be taken downstairs to the kitchen in the morning for wick trimming.

The tall piece of furniture was a new kind of bedroom furniture in this era. An interior top shelf stored hats and bonnets while

interior wooden hooks allowed clothing to be hung and protected from dust for the first time ever. Enclosed closets were still rare in the middle class household until after the Civil War. Extra bedding has been stacked under the rafter wall and unless the walls are insulated with sawdust or mud, a chilly night could require an extra blanket.

The 19thC farm family saw lots of green and lots of brown in their daily life – lots of weeds and growing crops and lots of soil and barn timbers. No wonder they chose more color for their dwelling's interior. Most of the painted antique furniture, now highly prized by collectors, originated on a farm. So think of that hard working farm family when you buy that Prussian blue mule chest.

Not only were furniture pieces painted vivid colors but the dwelling's interior woodwork was also brightly painted.

Woven coverlets certainly added more color in a bedroom. There are two types of "coverlids". One type was a geometric pattern and could be loomed by the local weaver. The other coverlet type was woven at a later date on a Jacquard loom. This loom produced an overall elaborate design such as flowers, vines with a border of buildings, trains, horses or houses. These Jacquard looms were huge and stationary and were operated by trained weavers. The geometric coverlets were earlier but the Jacquards will draw the best price at auction, especially if the coverlet has a horse or train motif as a border.

A coverlet is even more valuable if the coverlet is marked with a name, date and county.

At the foot of this rope bed is a mustard geometric coverlet while the red and indigo coverlet is a Jacquard coverlet. In 1843 in Ohio, a geometric coverlet cost $3.00.

Typically, clothing was kept in a bedroom where it was hung on a peg rack or placed in a trunk. A peg rail, also called pegboard, was a standard element in the bedroom, kitchen and back entry.

A period homeowner today often desires peg rails in their new-built traditional house but seldom are they installed by period methods. Most modern peg rails are nailed into dry wall and studs as a wall accessory.

The peg rail installed in a house of post and beam construction was affixed during construction. Peg rails, floor baseboards and window woodwork were part of the post and beam construction and as such, plaster was drawn up to these elements thus making plaster and pegboard edges even.

In this construction method, a peg rail could be placed anywhere between two hewn or sawn uprights. In the modern home, the peg rail is best situated between two windows or between a doorframe and a room corner, rather than just anywhere on a wall.

If an authenticator installs a peg rail, it needs to be sturdy enough to hang your ancestor's heavy winter clothing, bags of saved seed corn, oats and flax seed, and a few extra ladderbacks – all of which could have been found in a rural 19thC bedroom.

And yes, next year's seed was stored in rural middle class bedrooms, safe from rodents.

Only one step into a bedroom is needed for an impression to be made by the brain. This bedroom sends many positive signals but also a tiny negative.

Here's why.

This four poster bedstead is admired because of its simplicity and its appropriately woven coverlet. Any telltale sharp edge of a modern mattress is masked and that is a good thing. Yet the accent pillows inform us the owner follows trends of professional decorators by layering many accent pillows at the head of the bed and that is a not such a good thing for period style bedrooms. Country and period homeowners need no help from New York City decorators. We kindred spirits create our own style by learning from the early housewife how she dressed a bed.

Think about this. A bedstead steals a huge portion of a room's square footage so that footage must send the right message and hint strongly what the room is all about, otherwise the room fails.

The best news is this homeowner has created a big dose of "believability" in the corner – a primitive youth bed with a framed document above. How can two minor objects turn a room into awesomeness? The answer is the central tenet of authenticating and it follows. We can read this corner scene like a book! The parents have a sick child so a chamber pot is under the bed. A cloth and extra night clothes on a chair are nearby.

There you have the story. Now the answer . When an authenticator creates a story with antique furnishings and objects, a very special space becomes noteworthy, even memorable, but it is the story that propels the room to its highest potential. Create believability in all your rooms by establishing daily life scenes that fit the room. Ask your '1830's pretend family' for help.

This bedchamber has several interesting features that offer lessons to novice authenticators. If a bedchamber was ample in size, it often had several pieces of furniture – this table for writing and reading, chairs for visitors, a large chest for bed coverings, bed sheets and cases, a huge linen bag for feathers, another bag for dirty clothes, a candle stand and a 'cupboard bed'.

In the foreground is a table covered with a woven table rug. It also has a book pillow. Books were mighty expensive being hand bound with a hand tooled leather cover. Hence for

centuries a book pillow was used in European monasteries to lessen any weakening of a book's spine. Here the book pillow is incorrectly constructed not allowing the book's spine to rest correctly, instead actually damaging the spine rather than supporting it.

In the background is the cupboard bed – a very old form aimed to keep drafts at bay and away from affluent sleepers.

This bedstead is surrounded by curtains on two sides and walls on the other two sides. It offered privacy for parents and some draft control. Wrought iron screws installed in the ceiling support rope or cord on which hangs two or three lengths of hand sewn linen or wool yardage. The bed curtains were fastened to the cord or rope by metal rings or linen tabs that tied loosely onto the cord. This type of bed would not be available to all sleepers in the household as the yardage was a big expense. Remember the period terms for the bed and its bedding are unlike the modern terms we use today. Read this chapter to understand these terms then use the terms to connect yourself to a past century. Better authenticating decisions are made when you connect yourself to the past.

This form of bed is called a press bed; it folds up against the wall to save daytime floor space. It was usually "set up" in back parlors, keeping rooms, even in early 1800's kitchens. Imagine three children sleeping in this press bed nightly!

When a press bed is listed in an old estate inventory, you can rightly guess many children once lived in a small dwelling.

The bedchamber was fitted out by more human labor than any room in the house. Not even the kitchen which may have fed a large family required the amount of labor as did the bedchamber. While a family could grow and preserve all of its annual food in six months; it took 12-24 months to produce wool and linen textiles for the bedchamber.

This curtained bed is a solution for cold walls, drafty floors and needed privacy. This bed of straw tick and feather ticks, its bolster and pillows, and the linsey-woolsey bed covering signal a correctly dressed bed for its era and the economic status of this authenticator's pretend household. The bed curtains hang from a rope with wrought rings. The head cloth is an indigo checked wool yardage hung over a persistently cold wall. A trundle or truckle bed is underneath. Often these old low-to-the-ground floor bedsteads had wheels to roll the bed out for a sleepy child. In fact the Old English word "tryndel" means wheel. A trundle bed under the right bed in the right bedchamber always adds to the story of that room.

Bedchambers through history served more than just one purpose. An authenticator's bedchamber will be more believable if the space illustrates several activities other than just sleeping. Here on the chamber wall is a tape loom often used near a bright bedchamber window. Clothing was stored and mended here. Stints of spinning and reeling could be a daily chore in this room. Creating work scenes is enjoyable and necessary if you are an authenticator.

One test of a wonderful authenticated room is whether it holds a surprise for our modern eyes. This bedchamber delivers that surprise after climbing a steep, steep staircase. Quick to behold is the first surprise – a curtained rope bedstead with side curtains hung by rope from the ceiling. Notice the bed curtains do not match; any yardage available in the household at the time of their making was good enough for a lesser bed upstairs. But beyond the bedstead was another surprise. That curtained bed is in an untidy room! Great! The room has been staged

"untidy" with clothes thrown carelessly over furniture and floor as planned by a serious authenticator! What fun! It is the untidiness that makes this room so believable, so true to daily life two centuries ago.

Notice the chamber's wall are put to use with shelves and pegboard – a good substitute for a furniture piece. Hence, clothing hangs on pegboards; bedding is stored on wall shelves. An upper bedchamber can be awesome without expensive cased furniture pieces.

Linger here with your eyes wide open. You are looking at an authentic decorated room.

A second story bedchamber could be a work place also, so spinning wool is performed here after the fall harvest. Carded wool and wool roving are stored in large linen bags on the floor. An adjustable swift clamped to a work table was "fitted" with hanks of spun yarn to be wound off into skeins or balls which then made the yarn ready for knitting. Mending was done near the bright window; short gowns, shifts and shirts, and breeches were sewn here in spare time. Wool clothes were aired on the line; other clothing dried here in the winter. Even the heavy feather tick, weighing 25 to 40 pounds, was shaken outdoors to redistribute the contents or aired indoors in winter on a rope line.

Attend local "Sheep to Shawl" events to buy your raw wool supplies. These happenings are usually sponsored by county sheep improvement associations or by a spinning and weaving guild.

This chamber speaks volumes with every element having a purpose being in this rural bedchamber. This statement is a major tenet of authenticating. If an authenticator can not justify an object being in a particular room, the object has no reason being in the room. And if in doubt as to whether or not an object is in its rightful place, ask a knowledgeable friend or a period home consultant.

The bed here has a buffalo skin bedcover and has linen bedsheets and cases. A redware chamber pot is safe under the bed from accidental spilling; after its use it was covered with a small piece of tow or "checker'd stuff" which helped contain odor. The blanket crane holds an extra bedcover, a spare bolster. The long linen nightshirt on the wall was probably hand sewn similarly from a work shirt pattern. A blanket crane draws the eye to the ceiling which is a good thing. The fireplace has a handy cupboard above; it's an "in-wall" cupboard constructed between wall studs. If the reader has a boring wall, an "in-wall" cupboard could save the wall from boredom.

Opposite the bedstead is a clothespress, an old term for any receptacle for clothing. Depending on the era and region a clothespress could be a closet, a chest, or a wardrobe. This clothespress is a wood frame with navy wool yardage attached. A toilet cloth usually covered the top for dust control but here an oriental rug fulfills that purpose. Sometimes a length of chain was inserted into the bottom hem to keep the fabric on the floor and stop dust drifting inwardly.

Nearby the clothespress is a trestle table and a ladderback armchair. A document box, leather bound dictionary, a couple beribboned deeds and an agricultural tract are laid out for reviewing by the head of household. On the wall directly above is a framed 1700's land deed and an old map which must be highly prized by the male property owner. There is a lesson for authenticators in this scene. Do not mat framed prints, documents or artwork. Matting is a modern treatment. Use archival buttons that keep the glass off the exhibited work.

Another lesson is this. For many authenticators, a strong depiction of a male presence in their created period home is greatly lacking. Maybe it is lacking because the today's female very often plans the decor. But if an authenticator is serious about simulating daily life of the 1700s or early 1800s in their décor, then the male image must be very noticeable in that decor. Especially in middle class scenarios, the activities of father and sons certainly imprinted the early household. These male activities should be evident through their clothing, tools, religion, land ownership, community standing, and their ancestral heritage. It is so easy to show a woman's presence in a period authenticated home. It is more difficult to illustrate same for a male presence. When a male presence is not evident in a period home, that interior then tells only half a story.

A second story bedroom was often a catch-all for lesser or outdated furniture in middle class households. The primitive candle stand in this view is the earliest piece in the room. We can imagine it was once in an 1800 Ohio log dwelling. The bedstead is early to mid-1800s while the night gown is late 1800s. This homeowner has staged this upper bedroom with mixed furnishings as it would have been in a middle class dwelling.

Take a closer look. Observe the manner in which the bed is dressed. There's no modern mattress obvious here OR if there is a modern mattress it is well disguised. A fluffed bed tick filled with feathers or curled corn husks gives this bed a rumpled aspect which is accurate for the era of roped bedsteads. While most 21stC sleepers would not rest on such a bed today, an authenticator could duplicate this scene on a rope bed in a spare bedroom. An antique rope bedstead fitted with a 21stC mattress and foam pillows will always appear incongruous unless some disguising takes place.

The bolster and bed tick are constructed of "ticking", commonly a blue and white striped cotton twilled fabric used especially for ticks because of its strength.

In the heyday of roped bedsteads, the bolster was absolutely necessary. Its purpose was to fill-in the low spot which occurred at the bedstead's headboard when a plump bed tick was placed on the bed. The bolster, heavily stuffed, was topped with feather bed pillows which raised a sleepy head out of the low recess. The bolster was as long as the bed was wide and often was tied twice at each end with narrow linen tape.

This photo depicts a bolster correctly sewn as one piece but should be more firmly stuffed. It appears being used here as a long soft bed pillow which is not its purpose.

Some rope beds have a 'blanket roller' at the foot of the bedstead. This lathe turned horizontal wood piece between the two foot posts allowed a blanket to be attached, rolled and stored on it. What a good idea! On a cold night, the blanket's edge was grabbed and pulled over the bedding for more warmth without getting out of bed. If this horizontal piece turns easily on your rope bed, sew a blanket edge onto itself around the roller then wind the blanket onto the roller.

Visitors will find it is a curious item. When visitors have questions about objects viewed in your period home, take advantage of this opportunity to teach about daily life long ago.

Bed chambers, bedrooms are favored spaces for this writer because no other room has such a poignant purpose as a bedroom and when such a space is fitted with furnishings, those items must be perfectly defining.

In this view is a reproduced woven coverlet; its red color recalls the cochineal insect that in past centuries produced the red dye color before synthetic dyes were developed.

The pillowcases would be more believable if the red borders were removed and the ends were closed with 1/4-3/8 inch wide tape ties or old milk glass buttons.

The window covering is fancy enough for this "best bedroom"; it is plain, of simple style and is adjustable. Often a one panel sewn curtain has a buttonhole at a bottom corner and a button at the top diagonal corner to form the drape. The same could be accomplished with one woven tape piece attached at the bottom corner and the other tape piece sewn at the opposite upper corner then tied together.

There is one small concern with the lamp on the bedside table. Its crockery base is a reminder of the kitchen or pantry. Once that kitchen image reaches the mind it lowers the coherence of the bedroom. Substituting this lamp for one that relates to the iron strap fixture above would be an easy solution.

This writer's consultations with period homeowners often confront a bedroom or bedchamber problem. IMPORTANT! Often the problem is not the bedroom itself, nor are its furnishings at fault. The weakness lies in how the bedroom appears to our modern eyes. Time and again the concern discussed is the bedroom has been staged in the manner of a modern hotel room – two beds separated by a lamp stand. Our modern eyes recognize this hotel arrangement instantly and that 20th century influence tells one's mindset that something is amiss. The eye of the beholder becomes confused when inside the "hotel" room; something just does not seem right in such a period bedroom. Then a test is suggested and performed and when the bedsteads have been moved differently, sighs of relief win the day.

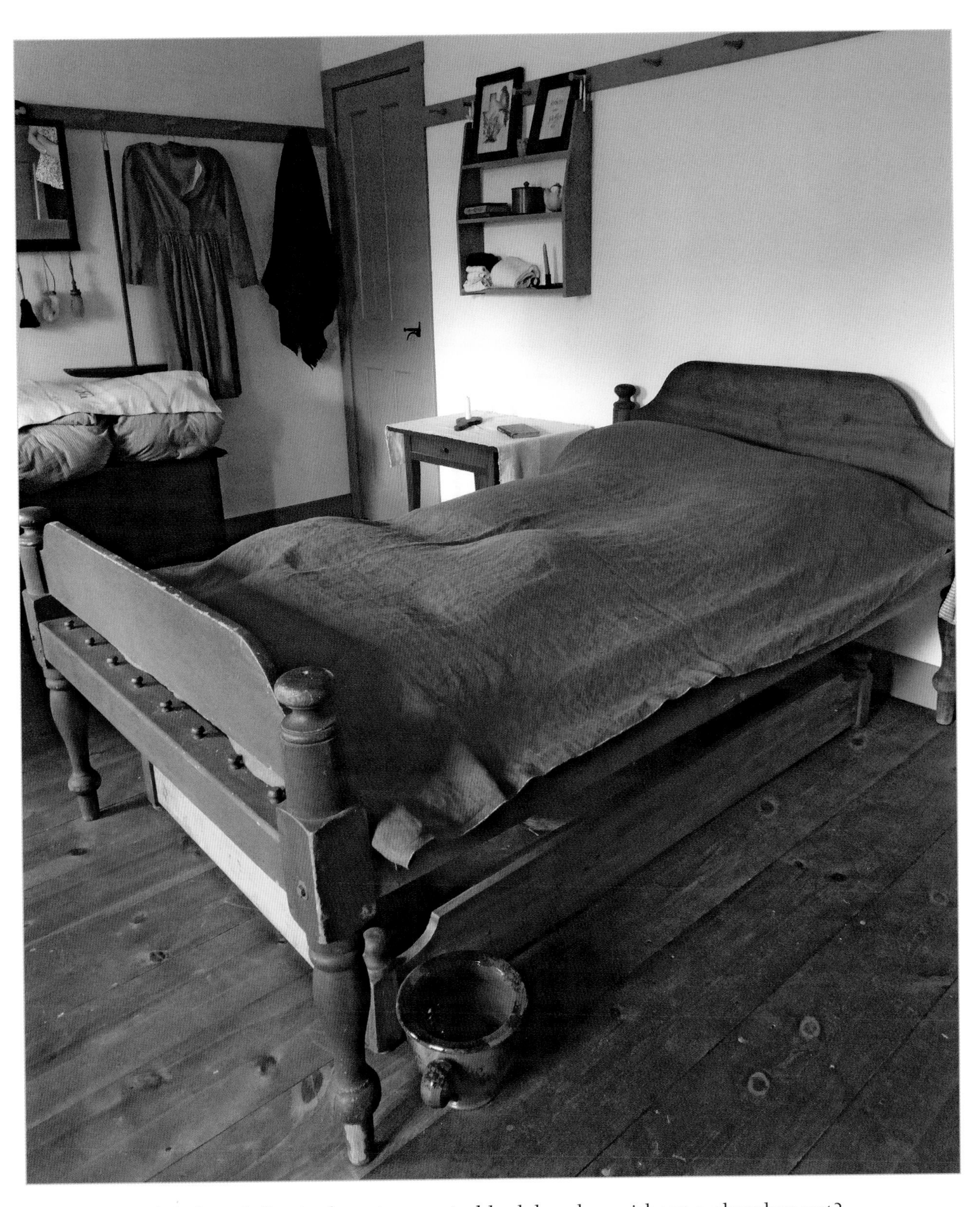

How much believability is there in a period bedchamber without a chamber pot?

This writer stated that question with much emphasis to a few Texas authenticators. They did soon order the reproduced redware chamber pots from "Henderson's Redware of Bangor Maine" as was suggested. The 18th and early 19thC goodwife placed a chamber pot sometimes in an upper hall outside of bedrooms, or under a bed or in a bedroom corner. The following morning the chamber pot would be cloth covered, if the household was genteel, to be carried through

the house and emptied outdoors. Lidded white ironstone chamber pots came to market in late 1800s so be smart to match era of chamber pot to era of your bedchamber.

Evidence of period clothing in a period bedroom must relate to the occupants who sleep in that chamber. These occupants are probably modern day family members BUT the room could be staged as if a "pretend family relative" was occupying the room. Clothing choice is important because the mind will be greatly confused if fancy Victorian clothing hangs in a staged "poor daughter's bedroom" or if young girl's period clothing appears in old Aunt Lida's bedchamber. So gender, economic status and age of the sleepers must be decided beforehand by the authenticator. Why is this small matter so important? It matters because diverse period clothing is the driver for each bedroom being different and when each bedroom is totally different that makes bedrooms exciting in your home.

Middle class bedrooms of the past had only a few components: a bedstead, bedding, a chair, a chest and some articles of clothing. Most kindred spirits would judge such a bedchamber as boring. The authenticator can avoid bedroom boredom by staging each chamber very differently. If staged well, no authenticator would ever use the contemporary words, 'master suite' or 'son's bedroom' to describe any bedroom in your dwelling! It does take a new mindset, discipline and determination. So erect that four poster, bring in an early desk, a simple wing chair, and add some 1700's clothing. It does not matter whether these furnishings are reproduced or antique; what matters is that this bedchamber is "totally different" from the others in the household.

Try staging a son's room as a hired man's room or a spare bedroom as an 'elderly uncle's room'. Specific period clothing is the heart of a "wonderful to view" bedchamber.

Authenticating is all about creating a period room as believable as possible. Believability is accomplished often with textiles placed such as an early housewife would have needed them. Here in this view is a bedroll on top of a dovetailed walnut blanket chest. The bed tick is rolled and tied for summer storage. Summer sleepers in the past shunned hot feather ticks for cooler straw ticks. Here we can imagine an 1840s middling family having no designated cupboard nor a large splint basket for feather bed storage so it is placed on the chest and covered with a coarse tow sheet. With two rope beds and four sleepers in this room, both feather and straw ticks "go flat" quickly and must be aired and shaken.

Airing, refilling and storing all the bed sacks each spring and fall is a week's work for all females in the dwelling.

Our modern mindset forces today's homemakers to think every bedroom must be furnished with today's trends as much as funds allow. Not so for upper story bedrooms of the middle class centuries ago. Upper bedchambers were often supplied with cast off furnishings, old outdated bedsteads, worn bed linens and it got worse in low income bedrooms where one would find flat smelly feather pillows or a pillow stuffed with bran, blankets with holes, and only a nail to hang clothing.

This upper bedroom has been made lesser by a skin laid for a floor rug, a very old Delaware Valley armchair, and no curtain on the storage shelves which the genteel set in the city would have installed over all the baskets. One thing is for sure. When bedrooms are planned each to be different, it adds adventure room by room.

Just make sure the homework is done and the result is scrutinized diligently.

New homes built in the 1970s often had bedroom closets with bifold doors.

Dismantle those as soon as possible. It's easily done in minutes and a basket closet can be yours. A basket closet makes good storage for bedding and out of season clothing.

Any basket filled with modern articles can be covered with a woven checked cloth – hand hemmed of course.

The box bed in this view was common in early German homes because of its very simple construction and available wide boards sawn from their farm's old tree stand. German farmers were thrifty by culture; hence no need for head or foot bed boards. A cornhusk bed sack was laid on slats across a thirty inch high box bed. The bed sack was then topped with a straw or feather tick for comfort, all high above floor drafts.

Above this box bed are two swivel blanket cranes from which bolster cases, linen bedsheets and especially blankets could be hung at arm's length of the sleeper in case an extra blanket would be needed.

German farmers worked hard but they slept comfortably.

German farmers were the best agriculturalists in early America. They had an advantage from their earliest arrival in the 1600s as they knew how to choose farmland from their European ancestors. Wherever the hardwood trees grew tall and strong, that is where corn grows best. Hence German home interiors usually had walnut wood work, unpainted for generations. If only softwoods were available for their home's interior use, it was painted to hide its inferiority. Hence this bedroom's woodwork is painted.

A wooden hanger for multiple shirts and black braces, the period word for suspenders, hang from the pegrail. A redware chamberpot already has its genteel cloth wrapped in the handle. A wide brim felted Mennonite hat hangs from a peg. A gusseted muslin shirt has seen many hot days in the haymow. A blue and white checked curtain turns a wall recess into a clothes press.

Chapter 2

The Work Room or Kitchen

Sometimes a room corner is so boring that the eye has no reason to return to it; however this kitchen corner attracts the eye readily. Boring corners are referred to as "dead corners" by this writer because they contribute nothing to the success of the room.

In this photo, the handsome wall cupboard is NOT staged with a collection! Instead its "near at hand contents" are used daily by the homeowner and that brings believability to this kitchen corner – which is a very good thing!

Sinks in today's period kitchens are best if of a dark substance such as aged copper, soapstone or a black silgranite. This sink base is simply constructed with no toe kick area. Kitchen base cupboards with a toe kick area can be improved by installing stained or painted wood blocks shaped as "legs" under a few or each base cupboard. It's an easy improvement for a handyman.

Walls and ceilings should be useable space because the early housewife certainly put them to use. When any room lacks marveling, these surfaces are begging for some eye attractions.

Here is a table which serves as a work surface. In past centuries large kitchens hosted several work tables which is still a good idea today instead of a modern "island". The overhead joists and hung objects attract the eye upward; every room needs to attract the eye up, especially in period kitchens. Bulk staples such as cornmeal, dried beans and peas, flour and salt are hung in tow sacks from the joists. A modern "cooler" is masked behind a curtain.

Sometimes a single cupboard on a wall can appear lost and disconnected from the remainder of the room. However, thanks to the large red firkin it is saved of that moniker. But the firkin does more. It takes the eye higher and beyond to the handsome ceiling beam and that is a good thing. This kitchen cupboard was once the principal player in foodstuff preservation. To authenticate this area, visual signs of those chores could be presented here. For example, a basket for retrieving potatoes from the cellar, a checked hand sewn apron hung on the cupboard's side, a cotton-tied bag marked "rice" could join the firkin. The wooden box of apples on the floor nearby announces apple dumplings for supper.

An authenticator will liven up an area with a work scene to give it a more believable presentation.

Faux foodstuffs are not objectionable to this writer but poorly produced faux food is; more so when faux food is displayed where real food never would have been presented. So be smart. Buy good quality faux food and place it in a truth spot – in other words – where it belongs.

This kitchen corner exhibits several features that override its modern components. The wood countertop adds more wood surfaces to the kitchen scene. A red cupboard makes a strong finale at the end of the kitchen wall leaving wall space for a utilitarian shelf and pegboard. A kitchen always appears more spacious and of another era when wall space is not filled with a continuous run of cabinets. The galley board around the countertop lessens the harshness of what otherwise would have been a sharp countertop corner.

Authenticators will incorporate wood surfaces as much as possible and disguise kitchen appliances, large or small, behind wood panels or tension rod curtains. Build wood enclosures for refrigerators, microwaves and cook top stoves.

The contents of the brown painted wall cupboard hold a lesson. Open kitchen shelves must not appear as a showcase. An early cupboard would have had assorted items, as seen here, and this would have been more realistic.

Decorators would probably like the kitchen window curtained here but the authenticator knows a kitchen was always a work place needing light, work surfaces, few cupboards and no frills. The checked cotton towel put working hands in mind. Shelving provides both the early and present day housewife with reachable kitchen implements. Working in a kitchen with walls of shelving versus walls of upper cabinetry is pure refreshment.

Be brave and remove the lesser used of the upper continuous run cabinets. Then step back and feel the relief of not being overpowered by them.

Both country style decorators and period home authenticators admire chandeliers. Country home decorators are under no rules where a chandelier should be hung so here a chandelier in a kitchen is pleasingly dramatic.

However for the period home, a chandelier in the kitchen, always known as the work place, is incongruous. It should never be equal to a similar one in the next room as seen in this view. In the foreground, the timbered upright beam is handsome and could stand alone unadorned. Always accentuate the positive features of a room and lessen the negatives. The authenticator would allow the patina of the upright beam to speak for itself. Sometimes even a positive element needs a tweak to make it awesome beyond the positive note.

Enhance the base cabinets with legs so that they appear to be free standing units. If the cabinets are already installed, add some blocks of wood, styled simply as cabinet legs. Cut them to the depth of the toe-kick area, paint them to match the cabinets and glue them in place. Try this to one or two select cabinets.

As country decorators, many of us treasure the dry sink which became common in rural households about 1850. Our inherent inclination is to place it in a room where we can best admire its simple lines or beauty of its surface whether it is painted or untouched.

This kitchen dry sink, above left, knows that it is opinionated and knows that it is well made and has a good looking body but it resides in a sitting room which is disheartening. While it is thankful for the nice window view and good company of stone crocks, it desires most to be in the kitchen with the relatives.

A dry sink in the 19thC was invaluable to the housewife and was a necessary tool for the operation of the family rather than a piece of furniture to be admired and adorned. It was the work horse of the mid-19thC kitchen.

In an authentic dwelling, the dry sink would have been placed where it was used in its day. To authenticate, it is a good idea to follow the old adage – have a place for everything and everything in its place.

In the foreground is a wooden bowl. Great- great grandmother would have advised after cleaning a wooden bowl with a damp cloth, the bowl be placed on a flat surface upside down AND with its rim over the table edge for the moisture to escape – this procedure limited warping. Notice the pantry is just a couple steps away from the kitchen. The wall box is handy from the sawbuck work table.

A work table should be prominent in 19thC kitchens. They were the countertops of their era, usually set in front of a 1700's fire or under a window of an early 1800's kitchen as seen here.

To the left is a green painted baker's table which was a new kitchen helper by 1850. This fine example certainly brought convenience to the cook. The front bottom drawers were wood-faced but the flour bin below was tin. The top was zinc which was the first non-porous work surface for the middle class kitchen. The more affluent housewife could afford a copper work surface.

Placing objects where the housewife long ago would have used them is a sure way to authenticate your room.

There are rooms that speak not about the early housewife but of the collector. The two worlds are miles apart but both are exciting.

The collection of wooden bowls has been placed as a display set on edge to attract the eye. The lighting is candle or candle-like power which is a good thing.

But the chandelier over the meal table relates to a very formal dining room juxtaposed to the country kitchen furnishings which the housewife enjoys by incorporating both worlds as a decorator. Two camps exist – those that follow history and the early family's activities and the other camp which follows their desires and the adventure of collecting. But both camps form a common thread. We all enjoy gathering antiques and we are good stewards until the next generation purchases them.

The subject of table cloths or table coverings is rare among the today's kindred spirits. After all, it would be shameful to purchase a handsome wide board table then cover it. Right?

Table coverings for meals or dining tables were common since the earliest settlements of the English Pilgrims, settlers of the Plimoth Colony in 1620. This genteel act lasted for 330 years! Finally table cloths on the dining table expired about 1950 when the vogue of placemats and mahogany furniture appeared. Not only should all tables be covered, so should a parlor tea table, a bedside table, a game table and a sewing table. This was a custom for centuries in homes of all social classes except the very poor. Isn't it ironic that some period homeowners today display their tables bare as the poor once did?

Today if authenticators are striving to represent any era of those 330 years, should we not also resurrect the table covering to reappear on our beloved antique bare wide board tables?

Please sew it of white linen with narrow hem!

Dry sinks were common in American urban kitchens by the Civil War and were still popular in rural homes in the late 1880s. The dry sink was constructed in different regional forms but the most common was a wood cabinet with storage below and a recessed area above which was lined with zinc, tin or copper. Often painted, dish washing, vegetable prep and meat cutting took place in the sink well, while cutlery, utensils were kept in a small side drawer. Waste water was drained through a pipe to outside or carried outside with a dishpan or bucket. Before the dry sink appeared, the cook prepared all meals and washed all cooking vessels and dinner plates in a tin dishpan on a work table placed before the fireplace.

Here this red painted dry sink has an adapted water pump, a deep well and ample storage below. It is staged with a tin dishpan, a candle, dish cloth and towels. This authenticator has added a stoneware jar for soft soap, homemade scrubbers and slop pan. To the right of the dry sink are strings of apple slices drying.

A tin pierced lantern is a popular lighting device today in country and period homes. Often it is displayed where it should not be. An authenticator who has done some homework keeps this lantern in a working kitchen or at a back door entry; there it hangs in a handy and ready place.

Tin pierced lanterns were constructed to allow light to spread over a dark path at night and to keep the candle flame contained within its tin walls. At night time in the 18th and 19thC, a farmer needed to check livestock, a minister might need to guide a parishioner to his front door, a son must be sent out into the night for live coals from a neighbor.

Kitchens of the past were work places! The homeowner here has shown work activity in the drying of apples, herb harvesting, preserving and dish washing. The lantern is hung where it would be ready for any night event or emergency. Very seldom would a lantern creep deep into the household. It was lucky to get inside the back door.

An object placed where an early family would have used it is realism. Always strive for a realistic situation instead of a decorative one.

By the 1840-1850s, kitchen and parlor stoves were available even to rural folks, especially if a railroad was nearby. This six-plate heating stove with the surrounding foodstuffs is being kept warm during freezing temperatures. The early family here is of a progressive sort and has closed its fireplace for the modern stove. From this view it is easy to imagine eggs in a basket kept from freeze-cracking by the gentle heat of the stove, yeast kept alive in its redware pot, pumpkins curing for winter storage. Kernelless cobs stored in a hanging bag as handy fire starters. The churn is positioned for next morning's butter making. This modern day owner certainly has the mindset of an authenticator.

Can we of the 21stC ever realize the labor needed to spin wool for an entire family and its hired help for a year's wear and bedding? This work was done in an unused upper chamber or a first floor work room. In this photo is a spinning wheel compatible for producing wool single ply yarn. Other equipment was needed to form two or three ply yarns. An authenticator often has a wool spinning wheel in their home and it is often displayed in an unreal location. First, it must be near a well-lit window. The hands of the spinner, the maidens and orifice of the wheel must be in the stream of daylight. Also the wheel must be situated so that the spinner would

have faced the spinning mechanism without blocking the available light. Finally the spinner must have space for walking back and forth to draw out the wool fibers and return to allow the twist to go up the yarn. Hence a secondary name for wool wheel is the walking wheel. Identified parts of a wool wheel can be found online.

A serious authenticator will want their wool wheel staged as if a spinner just left her task. It is an exciting challenge for some period homeowner to see how true they can recreate the activity of wool spinning. Often country and period homes featured in periodicals depict a spinning wheel in an unrealistic position. When viewed, we then know the homeowners did not do their homework. Avoid being one of them as your home deserves better.

So, the wheels are being stored, not ready for spinning. Certainly the hired girl Lisbet will re-position her wheel in good light to begin her day's work. Lisbet is 14 years old and can easily spin five skeins of wool yarn a day walking back and forth over four miles while spinning at the 'great wheel'. One wool skein equals 560 yards. Lisbet would remark at the end of day 'I spun my spint', meaning she spun the number of skeins expected of her as a hired girl, while the lady of the house gains another 2800 yards of wool yarn for her weaving.

Every dwelling had a work space, or a work room; it could be a separate room in the back of the house or a space in an existing room. Here the big projects were started such as the picking-over of wool fleeces, the comb painting of a cupboard, giving haircuts to family members or producing felted wool by stomping it in a tub. Some of the activity in the work room required semi-permanent equipage like a quilting frame or a warping frame or an indoor clothesline. When touring an historic home, always view the work room and take notes; it is here that you learn how the early home really functioned.

The picture at left depicts a partial view of two rooms. The nearest room can be imagined as a front entrance hall. A couple of wool cloaks and a man's greatcoat hang at the end of the hall. At the back of the house, often was a workroom and here it is - the spinning room. Imagine entering the home's front door, walking its hall to the end and discovering the work room. When rooms are sharply defined as is this hall and spinning room, the home becomes adventuresome.

Collections are always a concern in period homes. Here the homeowner collects wooden dough bowls and is wise to contain them in one place on a suitable bucket bench rather than displaying them throughout the home in rooms where they do not belong. An 18th or early 19thC homemaker would have no need for all the dough bowls pictured here. Her bowls were few in number, were of different sizes, and when clean and air-dried, were stored on a shelf below her kitchen work table. Unless a period home has controlled humidity all year, wooden bowls should not be stored on edge. Store them upside down on a flat surface to even the pressure as wood reacts to different humidity levels.

The red painted cupboard has found a good home and the nearby pantry gives it good company. The homeowner clearly is disciplined because the pantry displays only pantry vessels and food storage containers. This spectacular red cupboard needs no additional adornment on its door.

It is a common practice of country decorators to open a cupboard door and hang an herbal wreath, apron or candle on the door's interior. However the early housewife had real reasons to keep her cupboard doors closed. She had flies, mice, mold to abate from her cupboard. She also had freshness of baked goods to keep in her cupboard. A period room appears less showy, less exhibitive and more real when cupboard doors are closed and not decorated with wreaths. In addition, a visitor's curiosity is peaked when cupboard doors are closed and that is a good thing.

Period homeowners aim to hide or disguise all modern elements in their kitchens. This kitchen illustrates the importance of wood surfaces with its wood countertops and dough boards to cover sinks and cooktops. Eliminating or reducing the number of upper wall cabinets produces a simpler and sparser space. Shelving is more believable in period kitchens than upper wall cabinets.

Think of the early cook and her daughters cooking in their kitchen. They prepared vegetables, meats, beverages, baked goods – the same comestibles we of the 21stC prepare but they had less aids. Surely the modern cook will not forfeit modern convenience but hiding or disguising these aids is doable and necessary. There are better ways to disguise a modern cookstove than using breadboards.

Here are some help points for a sparser kitchen. Only a few baskets, wooden bowls, firkins, pieces of redware or yellowware are needed; interchange and store the rest. An early kitchen was a work space. To show that aspect, remove kitchen curtains and decorative lampshades, decorative wall objects and any kitchen needless items. Sparsing is a good thing. Do question whether your kitchen and its era should have a floorcloth. If not, remove it and let the wood floor dominate.

Here's an opportunity to discuss those electric lamps with country style shades. While a country decorator is attracted to colorful lampshades, the authenticator must be more selective. Our modern eyes recognize a lamp as being electrical or kerosene fueled which already is a negative in an end 19thC mindset. To add a decorative lampshade to an electrical or kerosene lamp just adds to the fallacy. There are electrified tin lamps now available that are delicately designed to appear old with aged tin shades. Electrical lamps are necessary but authenticators do not want to emphasize their electrical parts by drawing the eye to a very attractive shade. So discard the eye catching shade. Always minimize the negatives and accent the positives in your period lighting choices.

Our eye is drawn immediately to the lovely period blue cupboard even though a work table is in the foreground. Many country decorators are not put off by a modern appliance in the kitchen such as a refrigerator. The authenticator, on the other hand, would most likely choose to disguise it with a wood housing so that the large modern necessity such as a refrigerator would not demean the period kitchen.

Some period homeowners place all electrical appliances out of sight behind a kitchen half-wall installed floor to ceiling. Another solution is placing modern kitchen appliances in a handy small connected room which allows the kitchen a true older appearance.

Here's a fireplace with a cooking hearth and a bake oven that in its day would have cooked food, preserved winter provisions and provided heat for the entire first floor. This fireplace was indeed a work horse but was coddled by a respectful housewife. It appears to be in a dining room but since it is a cooking fireplace, let's re-stage it for a kitchen work.

Starting from the hearth, there is a three gallon crock much too close to any fire in the firebox as crockery can stand heat but if cooled too quickly can crack. The hearth itself could be wider for the toaster and apple cooker. The andirons are good enough but the ash bed should be accumulatively deeper to hold embers overnight. The bake oven has a good iron door but where is the split wood?

The mantel is fitted out for a pewter show. The early cook would not have placed it so nicely, but any item that saves the cook extra steps needs to be kept handy. Here instead could be placed a pretend pot of bacon grease, crock of salt, pepper grinder, turning fork, a horn of spills, the copper measures, small trivets. And maybe husband can fix a kettle crane inside the firebox. Pargeting, re-plastering of the firebox, is a summer job.

The kitchen did not fare well for generations. It was the last space in the dwelling to be updated, repainted, improved, or to receive any new equipment. It was the work place of all workplaces – especially on the farm!

This kitchen view is of a better than average income family so it sports an easy-to-clean floor cloth. There is a fireplace with all the equipage needed for cooking country fare. This housewife must have reason to keep sun out of her kitchen as most neighbors at this time in history have no kitchen curtains. There is an inordinate number of wooden bowls. No early housewife needed that many but maybe her daughter is planning marriage. Who knows? The candled device hanging from the ceiling certainly looks expensive; such has been seen only in the county seat's courtroom in its day. The cake crock on the table will be empty by eventide. Does any one person know how this 19thC housewife keeps these walls so white? Most walls in the neighborhood are sooty.

This primitive kitchen has all the basic ingredients for a log dwelling. One cupboard for a few dishes, knives and spoons and horn cups with other shelves for prepared foodstuffs. There is a blanket crane over the mantel for drying clothes, blankets, and dishtowels. If the crane is long enough, a large center-seamed bedsheet will keep a tub bather privately shielded before the fire.

The work table has a raised lipped edge perfect for keeping ground cornmeal on the table instead of on the floor. It gets hard use multiple times a day – sorting beans, kneading dough, cutting vegetables and meat for stew, and teaching youngsters to print their name in leftover bran. The family meal is served here; the parents sit, the children stand. Dish washing is quickly done "put away" with hot water from the fireplace kettle.

Log cabins on the frontier had dark interiors – luckily this frontier wife has a window which aids her daily spinning stint.

We see such a small part of this kitchen but many lessons can be learned here. First, no distracting upper cabinetry exists but a good wall shelf is installed. This housewife knows the value of incorporating 100% cotton or linen textiles in her kitchen such as dish toweling. The wall shelf could house cloth napkins or drawstring bags of rice or beans. More textiles could be visible such as a couple of linen bags, tied or with a drawstring could be hung from the ceiling or a stack of large hand-hemmed napkins could be placed on the counter.

There is another lesson to be learned. Wood countertops will never be outdated. Hard to detect in this photo is the horizontal painted wood plank wall which is tight fitting, shiplapped or tongue and grooved. It is easier to paint a wood wall than to remove an outdated tiled back slash.

Aim for plastered walls, board or log walls in a kitchen; the effect is worth the effort!

Even better, use a glaze such as Ralph Lauren Tobacco stain applied over the plaster to further age the walls.

Who would deny working in this spacious kitchen? Plus the beamed ceiling, the hidden utilities and disguised modern appliances are all agreeable for a great country kitchen.

A red cupboard attracts the eye taking the viewer to the farthest wall. The eye always wants to see something interesting at the end of a view and the red cupboard fulfills that desire. The simple sawbuck table is situated for breakfast and bird watching. Notice a ceiling loft in the picture right.

Here the eye can travel through and out of the kitchen and into another room. The eye is happy with this kitchen. Remember how important it is for the eye to have reason to travel up? Here the eye has a real reason to do just that! The floored ceiling loft is above the kitchen dresser and is loaded with kitchen staples. The loft is the main attraction of this kitchen! Successful rooms draw the eye up.

This dresser is a working piece meaning its contents are used daily; the contents are not a collection displayed for show. For sure, many decorators would be tempted to use such a great open cupboard for a fabulous collection but this authenticator strives for authenticating, not decorating, and knows the dresser is more believable when daily used kitchen items are placed there. An early housewife would have done the same. "Well done" to the homeowner.

A stone sink is worth any installing effort in a period kitchen, be it old granite or new soapstone is of no concern. No matter whether it is plumbed modern or not, it has great influence in a pantry or kitchen. Visualize yourself at this non-plumbed stone sink with a tin dishpan rinsing fresh pea pods.

Approaching this enclosed dooryard, a visitor immediately notices evidence of work – chores daily performed by an 1820 housewife. Her "mornin' wash" has already begun and stints of wood chopping will be done by lamp time. There's a barrel top for plucking chickens and another barrel for catching rainwater. The nearby window allows ventilation through the home's interior; a "stay-stick" secures it from any night time entry. Early windows had no locking hardware. The entrance door is recessed under the roof – a godsend in time of blizzards.

This modern day homeowner is an active authenticator inside and outside the home. Evidence of landscaping this property in the 21stC trend is non-existent. Instead outdoor authenticated work scenes of the 1820s bring believability to the property as is evident in this dooryard.

This work room is a lean-to on the backside of an old Ohio dwelling. Two window-like openings in a plank exterior wall, each with a hinged plank closure, opens the work room to the outdoors without screen or glass. Myriad tools hang in various places: scythe, rake, wooden shovel, hoe, shoulder yoke and candle molds. Storage containers of every kind are overhead and roundabout: kindred baskets, a kilderkin, several firkins, a wooden well bucket, field canteen, nail keg, two chrome yellow barrels storing ground corn for winter chicken feed, a wooden tub for soaking a fleece, and several large tow sacks of sorted cornhusks. Gourds hang from the rafters for winter jackknifeing and tawed skins and hides hang here and there. Straw covers the floor year round for winter insulation, spring mud and summer dirt. A bucket bench is a space-saver keeping some buckets and pails off the floor.

A work room was not only a storage space, it was a family work place in past centuries. Here is where the dirty work of sorting and cleaning flax and wool took place, where the family's leather boots were oiled, and the tallow was strained of dregs. In summer, armloads of herbs came in while their refuse went out and the resultant tied herb bunches turned the ceiling rafters green.

If an authenticator has a anteroom near a back entry, create a work room of it. Sometimes entering a dwelling thru the back door is more exciting than entering through the front door!

A visitor would be readily attracted to the beamed ceiling but the floor cloth is begging for attention also. Some homeowners would see the floor cloth as a purely decorative element but veteran authenticators know a painted floor covering offered benefits to the cook in the kitchen. Babies played on them, spilled food was easy to clean up and their colorful designs added cheer in the room. This particular floor cloth is too fancy and too decorative for a working kitchen but would be suitable in a middle class sitting room or front hall.

A floor cloth painted in one solid color would have fulfilled the needs of any early kitchen even in wealthy homes. Presidents Thomas Jefferson and John Adams had solid green painted floor canvases in their kitchens. If more than one floor cloth exists in an authenticated home, the plain one should be in a work area such as a kitchen; the decorative one should be in the most public room – a parlor or sitting room. The floor cloth diminished in popularity about 1850-60 when linoleum was developed.

This kitchen fireplace is well-staged with appropriate tools and equipment. The mantel "stores" pewter for table use. For centuries the fireplace was the only indoor cooking source for a family's food until about 1840s in rural areas when a cook stove became available to middle class households. We can surmise this housewife has closed the fireplace for the summer choosing instead to cook meals on a step cook stove, not seen here, which produced less heat

in the kitchen. Hence chairs have been placed temporarily on the hearth. To distract the eye from the blackened firebox, the lady of the house has set a bouquet of garden flowers. All housewives, no matter what century she lived, would desire some pleasurable things, such as garden flowers once in a while, to brighten their workplace.

An authenticator might drape damp socks over the fire screen to be dried by the fire.

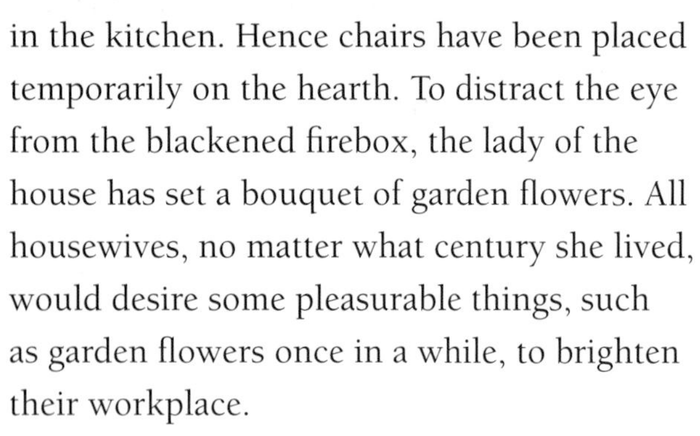

This view illustrates an important point of authenticating which is not every window needs curtains in an authenticated interior. There are no window coverings in this kitchen because for centuries the kitchen was a workplace. Today's housewives have been indoctrinated by professional interior decorators that every window needs a window treatment. The good wives of the past would object. Their notion was that window coverings were needed when a clear purpose was determined, not as a whim of fancy.

A curtain was needed to keep cold wintry drafts at bay, to divert hot sun during the dog days of summer, to prevent window peeking by city passers-by. The toil of spinning and weaving was endured only to produce curtains where necessary, not in the kitchen and other work spaces within the dwelling.

Often the farmhouse working kitchen and meal table area were one room. No separate dining room exists in a middle class home.

Here the kitchen end of the room is entered by the back door while the meal area at the other end can be accessed by early risers from the staircase. A long slide-extension table allows large family dinners to be held in the same space. On the farm, these kitchen extension tables were common by 1840s ingeniously pegged and constructed of walnut on Ohio German farmsteads.

The rural middle class housewife probably admired the fancy curtains of her genteel urban contemporaries but she hand-stitched simple curtains. The "one panel curtain" was favored for its simple construction but also for its multiple ways it could be "fixed". Pegboard here allows this one panel curtain to boast a somewhat genteel swag appearance, appropriate enough for a rural meal area.

Once a group of serious authenticators met for chat time and to style a one panel curtain in as many ways as five brains could design. Thirteen styles were devised. No wonder the rural housewife needed only one curtain style.

This curtain is hung by a heavy string in a sewn casing. The waxed string is knotted onto small wooden Shaker knobs drilled and glued at each end of the woodwork's face. Other correct ways to hang a one panel curtain are by tacking the top hemmed edge along the very top edge, not the face edge, of the window wood work, or by tacking it on a nail at each end of the woodwork which results in a "scoop appearance" as seen here.

Years ago this writer worked for a nonprofit 1840s farmhouse restoration. Finally it was time to install curtains in "the best room". The walnut woodwork was examined for nail holes where curtains might have been installed. No nail holes! Soon a step ladder helped to reveal a row of tiny tack holes in the very top flat edge of the woodwork. An entire chapter could be written about ways the 1800-1850s housewives "fixed" their one panel curtains.

In period home décor, it is not enough to have just suitable fabric for window coverings. The curtain must be constructed in a style also suitable to the chosen era of the room. Like clothing styles which come and go, window coverings changed styles as well.

The best of period window coverings follow these guidelines. Reproduced fabric is correctly chosen. The curtain style has been researched. The household's economic status has been considered and most important, the window covering has been hand sewn. When all these elements come together, these textiles bring a huge strength to the room. When these textiles are off the mark, the room never reaches its potential.

A middle class farmhouse meal table should be set differently than an urban middle class dining room table. Whether it is the dinner dishes, glassware or a centerpiece and tablecloth, these elements will announce clearly whether the diners are rural or city folks, or the meal an everyday meal or a holiday meal.

Here is a farmhouse kitchen table scenario. After a meal, dishes were washed in a dishpan in a dry sink nearby and returned back onto the table bypassing storage in a cupboard – the dishes were efficiently available for resetting the table again for supper! When an authenticator's mindset thinks "work scenes" rather than creating planned vignettes and tablescape, the kitchen or dining space is always more believable, more truthful to the activity of the early rural housewife.

Creating work scenes is a speciality of authenticators. Work scenes will always trump vignettes and tablescapes no matter what room the reader views.

The meal area of the rural kitchen has a wall shelf for empty tin candlesticks. They will be fitted with tapers from the back work room come candlelight, the period term for twilight.

This kitchen has several evidences of kitchen activity. The kitchen chest is an old case piece commonly found in rural pre1850 kitchens. It has primitive shaped legs and two hinged lid compartments for bagged flour and cornmeal storage. It was constructed with large corner dovetails. Grain painting is original. A young son on horseback would be sent to the mill for meal, enough to last the family six or eight weeks.

The red cupboard has a galley so the flour from pie and bread making can be somewhat contained. Girls were taught to knead dough at an early age.

The early housewife would be proud of her splendid copper ladles; the ladle cloth she added to quietly draw your attention to her best kitchen wares. This was a popular wall accessory in German kitchens. The kitchen corner cupboard stores colorful transfer ware and 1820s pink lustre dishes – both used as everyday table wares in 1800-1830. The hanging wall box holds newspapers, long out of date, but used to teach the children to read.

No other room in the dwelling produced the basic necessities of life as did the daily work executed in the early family kitchen. Often an authenticator needs only to remove some articles from the kitchen rather than add objects so that the more basic the period kitchen is, the more true to its era it will be.

Many 1850s middling class town and country kitchens had a staircase from the upper bedrooms down to the kitchen. Water came to the drysink from an outdoor pump nearby. Soft soap was near at hand in a crockery jar for dish washing. Fingers were dipped into the soft soap and then agitated in the water to produce suds. Clean dishes went back to the table after drying. Baked goods and foodstuffs for the next meal were stored in the pie safe.

The cubby hole on the stair wall served as a safe-keep originally, but here the candle light serves as a night light.

This room exhibits a mastery of a homeowner's discipline. Each and every object has its space; and there's wall space for the eye to rest. All objects here relate to kitchen chores – cupboards for comestibles, firkins for staples of flour, sugar and cornmeal, pantry boxes for tea and dried herbs. And the Shaker armchair? It is for the housewife who knits while the dinner cooks.

A sparse room is only attainable if the homeowner has discipline. Sparse rooms always photograph better.

Chapter 3

Hallways, Stairways and Small Rooms

A schoolmaster's desk or a miller's desk was never meant to have an accompanying chair. Business at school or at the mill was conducted on two feet. The desk's deep interior had storage for books, loose papers, accounts, mail, personal and small items needed at hand and a lunch sack.

This desk could also have been at the front entrance of a country lawyer's home. There the lawyer met his client, collected the fee and made a future appointment. The inkwell and quill are at the ready. The lantern is nearby to 'let in' the next client after dark. The scene could be authenticated further if artwork above was changed to an era friendly portrait of an American president or a document of an early law academy. Even a shelf for newspapers could replace the framed print.

In a period home seldom does an average piece of antique furniture stand well on its own meager merits. It needs related implements to make it speak.

All authenticators work diligently to remove weaknesses in their interior decor. This work goes faster with a camera lens; a camera view is always truthful. Take a photo of a room corner – is it boring? Take a photo of a busy area. Is it too cluttered? Take a photo of a case furniture piece and note if its purpose is obvious?

The decorator has done an exceptional job of displaying treasured pieces in clear view upon entering the house. However, the authenticator finds the photo view here confusing because of the unrelated objects being displayed – shoes, weaving shuttles, sunbonnets, wooden and tin buckets, herbs – all unrelated.

Sometimes period homeowners overlook the obvious wrongs because no ready solutions are in mind. Help can come from a digital camera. Take a photo of a troublesome spot in any room and instantly the camera's view delivers the truth that the eye may have missed. A photograph will reveal if the room space is well done or it needs help.

To reach the second story of an old dwelling required a staircase which was called by different names depending on its construction such as the turn back stairs, the winder, and the ladder stairs. An old staircase was narrow with high-risers. Dangerous? You bet for a child or any person carrying a lit candle!

Today the wall along the stairs interests us more than the staircase. There is usually a light switch at the top or bottom of the stairs. Disguise these with wallboxes if code will allow. A muralist can transform the wall into a landscape scene. A carpenter can open the wall and fit a small cupboard there. Large portraits of ancestors can grace the stair wall. A rural stairway was often painted wood. Lastly this staircase is usually a public area of the dwelling. Hence a good place for artwork but maybe not family photographs since it was a public place.

There is a bit of mystery behind a closed door which certainly brings out the curiosity in us. The early family's house allowed no such openness. The cat certainly was not wanted in the dairy room nor the cat's dead mouse dropped in the pantry.

Mystery created by closed doors yields curiosity and curiosity promotes adventure. A good old dwelling always is adventuresome, door by door.

Hallways serve as a public space in old dwellings. It gave the homeowner control. Some visitors were invited beyond the hall into the family's space. Other visitors were patrolled conducting their business no further than the hall.

The manner in which the hall was furnished demonstrated the economic status of the occupants. A narrow hall with an unimpressive staircase was probably middle class. A wide hall richly furnished with wall hung oil portraits, a chair or two, a side table and a grand staircase was built for an affluent family.

If your home claims a front hall, make the most of it. because it is indicative of a traditional home. Other hall furnishings could be a wall map above a side table, a rug or floor cloth, a wall shelf for a lighting device, a stenciled floor, a wall table for hat, gloves and calling cards. Choose these furnishings carefully to correspond with the era of your home because the hall gives visitors their first impression.

Chapter 4

The Buttery, Pantry and Larder

If a group of period homeowners were asked to define the words buttery and pantry, they might answer that the words have regional connotations but are synonymous.

For sure the origins of both words are ancient with the root of pantry "panis", meaning bread, being the oldest dating back to 2nd and 1stC BC in the language of ancient Rome. Roman armies spread their culture and Latin language widely. Before 1100 AD, the word "panetier", the servant of the bread, was used in Old French language. It is from the old Middle English (1100-1500 AD) word "panetrie" that the word pantry evolved. Today the word pantry by a modern dictionary describes it as a small room in which bread and other provisions, silverware and dishes are kept. A pantry and a buttery have been different spaces since ancient times.

Prior to 1100 AD, in the Old French language the word "bot" also "botte" was recorded which meant a cask. A large cask stored wine, beer or ale. A cask was barrel-like constructed with staves for holding liquids, especially wine and was stronger and larger than a barrel. Casks and barrels were necessary liquid containers in the early buttery. As this French word "botte" spread to England, the spelling changed to "butt" from the old Latin form 'butta' meaning a vessel or cask. Hence the word buttery is a room where the bot, botte, butta or butt was kept.

The word buttery arrived in America with the English in the 1600s and was already a word of old usage. Today the meaning has expanded by dictionary definition as a room or compartment in which wines, liquors and household provisions are kept. A buttery has never been related to the making of butter but butter, as a food provision, can be stored there.

For authenticators who are creating a buttery, adding a cask, barrel or any large vessel for holding liquids especially wine, is necessary. Whether these are filled with actual liquids or not is unimportant. Displaying a barrel, a cask or some vessels is paramount; otherwise without these containers you have instead created a pantry. In today's authenticated period home there should be a strong distinction as to whether food provisions are portrayed as being stored in a wine-beer-ale based buttery or in a bread-based pantry with provisions, dishes and silverware.

Remember, middling and wealthy homeowners had other small rooms within the house than just a buttery or pantry. There might have been a dairy room, a cheese curing room, a stove-wood room or a cool game room for hanging wild game that demanded the many wares that period authenticators now store or display in a larder or buttery.

Rethink your buttery; rethink your pantry and choose those wares carefully.

If ever a room could be accused of clutter, the pantry or a buttery certainly would be a candidate since myriad items are stored in a small space. The homeowner here has avoided the appearance of clutter in two ways. First walls and shelving are painted one color which makes the pantry appear larger. Second, baskets and small drawers hide small objects and doors enclose the strays. The staggering of shelf height adds eye adventure – how boring it would be if all shelving were the same level! For the enthusiast who enjoys all things primitive, a buttery or pantry constructed of old wood for the floor, ceiling or walls makes it more memorable.

But this wonderful painted pantry and its contents might all disappear if ever the candle wall sconce was lit.

An authenticator places objects in realistic places.

This larder has ample shelving and window for ventilation so necessary in the contemporary early 19thC farmhouse. More evidence of stored foodstuffs and bags of dried beans, cornmeal, hops, herbs hanging from the pantry's ceiling beams would add believability. This larder is nicely appointed but it lacks staging to its portrayed era. Maybe an old drawer added under an existing shelf for silverware would add believability.

The rug is not needed for this reason. First the early housewife would not risk a nice rug escaping damage in her pantry. But there is a better reason. In old dwellings each room was totally different, totally significant, totally purposeful from the preceding room. Rugs in the middling household were extras, not needfuls. They belonged only in certain rooms, and the pantry was not one of them.

The housewife supplying this pantry is a true authenticator. She stages the pantry then actually uses her pantry, probably daily as did the early "goodwife". We can all agree this housewife puts her "old" pantry to real use. Because this larder is a believable space to our eyes, its story is obvious.

The housewife returns to the pantry often at meal time for her own preserved fruits, vegetables, jams and jellies. Her meal bin is full and her myriad pantry boxes and pails store herbs, rice, dried beans and medicinals. The radish pods are pickling in the covered crock. Only bread is absent. The root word of pantry is "panis" meaning bread. A loaf or round of bread wrapped in a vinegar damp cloth would complete this pantry's contents. Any form of bread will do but would be more meaningful if the bread receipt, the period word for recipe, and the bread shape honored the type of bread made by your 18th or 19thC ancestors. Many books are now available on artisan breads to guide you.

Authenticators must have bread visible in their pantry. That bread can be real fresh bread, real dried bread or a faux bread made of resin. Bread must be obvious in a pantry.

This buttery's log walls certainly have appeal. There is space for a stone basin and multiple shelves. Notice that the shelving is diverse – some high, some low and spaced irregularly. This shelving arrangement excites the eye and makes best use of shelf space for odd shaped containers. The red barrel should emerge from its corner to a more dominant place in the buttery. It is the signature piece of a buttery.

There is much to ponder in this interesting view. Bread is readily seen here as it should be in all pantries since the 1600s. Brown bread was a standard staple in early America; with a prized recipe it is still delicious today. Congratulations to this homeowner who knows brown bread should be in her authenticated pantry. But the word pantry does not correctly describe this space as there is a barrel and maybe a keg or a cask also for ale or beer, the main beverage of America's frontier families.

Whenever a room stored barreled contents and food provisions, that space was termed a buttery, from the old root word "butt" as described within this chapter. The coarse linen cloth had multiple uses in a buttery. Of course as a towel but also as window covering when hot sun heated the buttery. It could be a quick carrier of raw vegetables to the kitchen work table or a cover protecting food.

Wood plank walls, the hewn joist beam and the whale-tail shelf brackets fascinate the arriving visitor. Colorful wares please the eye. Yelloware, Morton spongeware and redware add a contrast to woodenware. Some objects here were used outdoors but stored indoors like the large mortar and pestle on the floor which pulverized, cracked or made edible grains. Attaching the pestle's head outdoors to a tree limb with leather gave the worker a less tiresome chore. Quill feathers and beeswax candles are stored and prepared here until needed in other rooms.

Authenticators know it is important to create a reason in any room for the eye to travel up. Unseen to us are probably some bulkier objects in the loft above but the structure of the loft is all the eye requires to be content.

A wagoner and his goodwife migrated to the Ohio Country and quickly their timbered cabin became cramped. He constructed a space for storing winter provisions, a pantry loft. The ladder allows a safe climb for child or parent for retrieving needed staples such as tow sacks filled with parched corn, dried apples, beans or wild plums. Larger cloth sacks contain gathered accrns, hickory nuts and walnuts which are shelled as needed. The basket on the loft's floor holds roots of all kinds – sassafras, burdock, ginseng, dandelion for medicinal use. Tins of maple syrup and other tins of honeycombs are stored here. A slab of smoked bacon hangs over the loft's edge, easily available for slicing. Leaf tobacco is within reach of the ladder. The pantry loft saves valuable floor space in the cabin and keeps foodstuffs rodent free.

For the authenticator, the loft attracts the eye upward instantly to the ceiling – and that's a good thing.

Not all butteries, pantries and larders were rooms; later ones were closets adapted for the same purpose. Some were not even four walled rooms but rather were six-sided cupboards attached to the ceiling. Today the country decorator and the period homeowner attach the words "hanging buttery" or "hanging pantry" to these ceiling receptacles. The housewife of 18th and 19thC knew this convenience as "a safe". In American literature and legal estate inventories the word "safe" was commonly recorded, never as a hanging buttery or pantry.

A food safe had a wood frame with punched tin panels on five or six sides. After 1855, this wood frame could be covered with newly available wire screening. A door allowed entrance to one or two shelves on which were stored wine bottles and cloth wrapped foodstuffs. It was suspended from a ceiling joist or beam with rope, less often with chain or wire. A bread safe stored breads, pastry and food stuffs and was similarly constructed but lighter in weight.

A meat safe was built likewise but smaller without shelves. It had a hook under the topside to hang family sized chunks of meat enough for several meals; a dish underneath the meat caught any drippings. Old property appraisals record safes being in a buttery, pantry or kitchen. They were usually homemade and hung in a dwelling wherever ventilation and temperature could be checked.

Some pantries and butteries were large enough in which kitchen chores could be done; butter churning, turning aging cheese, trimming candle wicks, sorting dried beans on a large sorting tray, starting new vinegars with vinegar bees. If space allowed, bigger kitchen equipment could be stored and used here such as a barrel of vinegar or beer, a family size butter churn, a table-top wooden flour sifter, large wooden cheese tubs, blocks of yellow beeswax or a mouse-proof tin box of saved garden seed.

Log walls, shelving plenty enough and a barrel come together here for a primitive buttery. It is the barrel that designates this space as a buttery. A barrel's wine content served well for cooking and beverage use in early settlements where water quality was often questionable.

The barrel was a signature item in the buttery long ago but here it is treated as a secondary object topped with a nondescript wooden box. The barrel is important enough to have its own space under the painted wall shelves.

Objects for this buttery have been carefully selected proving the homeowner has done some homework. A few more items could be added for color: a few green glass onion bottles, a wine decanter, a few redware plates, one or two checked linen cloths and a tied linen bag of salt and another of dry beans. A buttery in an active early household was colorful.

If improvements were wanted for this buttery, the two shelving units could be joined along the window wall; at the present the small shelf unit appears as a lonely prop. Also, let the wood floor dominate. A bare floor without the braided rug will enhance the buttery at no extra cost.

Just one step into this quaint space certainly should arouse one's curiosity as to what is behind these doors. Curiosity causes a person to halt, ponder for a second and then proceed. Anything that causes a visitor to ponder is a positive.

For example, if the red pantry doors were already opened as you approached ,would you be as curious or have taken a second to ponder what old implements and traditional foodstuffs might be stored, ripening, aging behind within doors? A period room must arouse curiosity in our 21stC mind and closed cupboard doors surely makes one curious.

Most authenticators are proud of their pantry and will gladly explain the use of a pantry and its contents if a visitor asks. A pantry of past centuries was just one part of the household trilogy, words that is, bulk raw vegetables, fruits and grains binned in the cellar go to storage of foodstuffs and utensils in the pantry which go to cooked food for the meal table.

The broom hangs ready for any needed floor sweeping as a pantry must be kept clean and sweet smelling. A large wooden bowl is handy for carrying potatoes or apples from the pantry cupboard to the kitchen. The open window allows good daylight and exchange of fresh air into the pantry. There are two objects not needed in this pantry – the window curtain and the floor cloth since this is a pure utilitarian space.

The cupboard to the left might house the best silver, the best china, large platters and punch bowl, tablecloths and large napkins and maybe a tin reflector oven and seasonal implements like kettles and fruit drying racks.

Chapter 5

The Sitting Room or Parlor

When an easy chair, our modern word for wing chair, first appeared in a household, it declared the family was no longer upstart. Of course it was far more comfortable with a goose feather seat and draft deflecting panels or wings but it was a pricey object and did impress visitors.

Since a sitting room in this era often was planned to impress, the expensive accessories were displayed here such as: a brass candlestick, a soft paste bowl for sweets, a wine decanter and glasses, a few books and a pair of spectacles.

In this home the blanket crane is seen above the easy chair, but in its day it was a pure utilitarian device for a bedroom or keeping room. In the home of an early goodwife, this "swing arm" was needed in a bedroom over a bedroom fireplace to warm damp bedsheets and bedclothes or on a kitchen wall near a fireplace to keep handy and dry towels or wet outdoor clothing.

It is the cupboard that attracts the eye. The patina is striking against the plain wall. On close examination it holds many kitchen items; tin candle molds, pewter pitcher and platter, redware.

What a handsome fireplace! It is in a beamed ceiling sitting room with a group of ladderback chairs, a settee and low table before it. The low table is rightly situated for evening family tea, for mending or reading before the fireplace. One ladderback has been fitted in an old way with a back cushion filled with goosedown or wool roving and tied to the chair's finials to give comfort, especially to an elder family member.

Censuses by 1790 prove dwellings were usually multi-familial abodes. Authenticators should represent this multi-family arrangement in their restored homes with appropriate furnishings and appointments arranged for the extended family. It is a fun venture for authenticators to host a fictional person from the past in their homes. This activity can certainly add new insight into the early household. One serious authenticator in Texas arranges 1770s comfort for two "pretend" elderly aunts who dwell in a chamber of their saltbox house. The existence of "Aunt Hattie and Aunt Ettie" automatically, it seems, brings believability to their chamber and inspiration to the 21stC homeowner who "invited" the aunts. Hosting "pretend" family members challenges the mind and keeps decisions aimed to a particular time period and not elsewhere. This cushioned chair could be for Aunt Hattie's or Aunt Ettie's comfort.

A handsome fireplace needs a well appointed mantel befitting of its era. The lighted lantern on the mantel is ready for guiding a night time departing guest. Herbs are drying for breakfast tea and candlesticks stand prepared. The hooked rug, no doubt, is eye catching but in the era of this large fireplace would not have been a wall accessory.

This comfortable sitting room is also serviceable and clutter-free. The seating pattern invites good conversation. The room is further appealing because of the use of painted furniture and colorful upholstery added to all the brown and tan elements.

Note the mirror. From the earliest day, the lady of the dwelling knew well the importance of daylight in a room as her routine and her chores were scheduled around daylight. She also knew how a mirror could reflect daylight into any dim room. Here the mirror bounces daylight back into the room and makes the lamp's glow doubly visible. To the housewife of yesterday a mirror was for reflecting light just as much as it was for personal grooming.

The country decorator is anxious to display those found treasures we kindred spirits relish and does so without any conscious thought other than to place them in a spot of prominence. An authenticator will recognize those treasures as being objects belonging where they would be used. If you are striving for authentication, creating truths in a room should be a top priority in one's mindset. Does the reader recognize those objects which would be found elsewhere in the 18thC home? Remember this is a sitting room but the wooden bowls here were kitchen items years ago and the yarn winder would have been in a work place, not in a sitting room. Simply removing these items brings more truth to this sitting room and at no cost! How great is that?

Here is a mighty nice sitting room – good daylight "to the plenty", an easy care floorcloth, an "easy chair" and nearby a stretcher base table that is not at all happy with the social climber across the room. That would be the wood bench with crockery underneath.

Whenever a family could afford to build a space designated as a parlor, it was destined to be a showplace where the best accessories were displayed. Hence the parlor was seldom used except for a minister's visit, a wedding or funeral, meetings with officials, neighbors making courtship arrangements and so on. But in the rural home, the parlor could also be used for quilting bees, rag sewing events, wedding dress construction, a knitting frolic, and the room where Presbyterian church ladies would meet .

It was for these events the long table under the window was moved to the parlor's center for "ladies work" and much gossip. Maybe for these events the hobby horse was returned to a child's room for pleasure riding. Then hopefully stayed there permanently.

This cupboard, located on a common wall between a sitting room and a dining room, affords the 21stC homeowner a choice of items to place on the shelves. If the cupboard was located in a sitting room, the 21stC housewife should display items appropriate to a sitting room which was and is today a public space. Visitors, neighbors, business associates were welcomed here, and maybe offered liquid refreshment here. The authenticator would fill the cupboard's shelves with some books, a small document box or two, a map roll or maybe a shelf of Indian artifacts. A small stack of dishes for gingerbread and a cider pitcher might be placed on its flat surface. Because the cupboard rests also on the dining room wall, the redware and other kitchen ware within this cupboard are appropriate to the authenticator who might also wish for these pieces to be in the kitchen. Any time kitchen ware is present in a room other than a kitchen or pantry, the eye views that room as having uncertain purpose.

Uncertainty makes the eye move away to something better.

The seating in an early 1840's rural sitting room was considered well-arranged if all the seating encircled the room against the outer walls. It was a common way to entertain in that time period among the middle class. A table might be centered. One upholstered easy chair among wood chairs probably caused rumors to fly that the family was 'uppish' middle class. The non-uppish made their comfort by heavily padding wood rocking chairs and chair seats without incurring the cost of an expensive easy chair.

If this homeowner is an authenticator, removing the chest between the sofas to a bedroom to store extra blankets and bedding will fulfill its original purpose. The vacant space would then be allotted to a low table. In the early 19thC, a chest, especially a blanket chest, was seldom seen outside of a bedroom or storage room.

A fireplace, from the time it is constructed until the day it is demolished, is always the focal point of the room. Every brick of its structure can attest to that. It is the strongest dynamic of the room. For centuries it was the only source for heat as well as the means for the 'goodwife' to prepare most meals.

This housewife might rearrange the furniture grouping in this room to bring the fireplace back to its central focal point and give it the place of honor it would have held in an early 19thC dwelling.

Beginning in the 1930s, the fireplace held less importance when old coal or wood fireplaces were transformed into urban gas fireplaces.

Some middle class households in the past possessed better things than could be afforded but some household goods were inherited.

So here is a story line that could be used by the authenticator who has some upscale furnishings but they are in a middle class scenario. We can imagine here an inherited tall case clock, an ancestral oil painting, the "poor man's silver" and an oriental rug as inherited items. Parlor walls of a middle class home were often raw wide boards in rural areas. When funds became available, the planks were stained or stenciled. Painted or wall papered plank walls would come much later to keep up with the genteel set in the community.

There is a concern in this photo. To the left of the fireplace hang a skein of wool yarn and a couple hanks of spun flax yet no wool or flax spinning wheel is in sight. Authenticators often make the mistake of displaying objects in an unrelated space. Not only is there no spinning wheel in the room but the wool and flax have not yet been prepared into balls for knitting some evening in the parlor.

Yes, displaying spun wool and flax is only a small element of this parlor so why should a writer make an issue of it? The answer is – this is an example of a mistake that hinders a homeowner from becoming an authenticator. A homeowner who places spun wool and flax wherever desired with no thought or care of where the early housewife would have placed these items, is a decorator. The authenticator considers the early housewife and how she arranged her rooms. The authenticator desires an interior that is more believable, more realistic, more true to history. Hence the wool skein and the hanks of flax will be found in a work space where spinning was done, not in the public space of a parlor. When placing objects in a room, the best advice is do not place it until you know for sure where it must be!

Caution! Today's homeowners should never place flax near a burning fireplace as just one spark can ignite flammable flax. Many dwellings of the 1700s and early 1800s were destroyed by fire and children burned to death by flax being dried or stored near a fireplace.

An 1820s rural parlor was only as elegant as the farmer's funds and his goodwife's good taste could produce. The creator of this 1820s parlor practices authenticating with great enthusiasm. A parlor plan was formed decades ago and with careful purchasing over the years, this parlor is successful. When a room is well done it tells a story that is believable to all its visitors. Here's a possible account.

The pretend "1820s owner" of this parlor could have purchased the cased clock from a local family moving further west beyond Ohio. The easy chair came to the parlor as barter between a local cabinetmaker wanting one of the owner's cows. The heirloom table rug traveled to Ohio with the owner and still is protected with a linen cloth when tea is served.

If doubt arises while fitting out a room, ask a member of your "pretend family" for advice. A silly notion, you say? Try it and reap the benefits.

Many dwellings had two parlors. The front parlor, a public space, entertained guests, community officials and the pastor. The 'back parlor' served as a family space which in its day attracted family members after the day's work is done. The wife aimed for some embroidery come eventide; two candles gave her ample light. A problem lately arose with critters marching across the floor so wormwood and tansy has been scattered. In another month, the summer fire board will be removed from the fireplace and then comes winter.

The old rocker chair has been in this house for several generations. Its smooth gaited rocking and comfortable seat are appreciated by all family members. With winter coming, knitting needles will be clicking in rhythm with the creaking sound of the rocker.

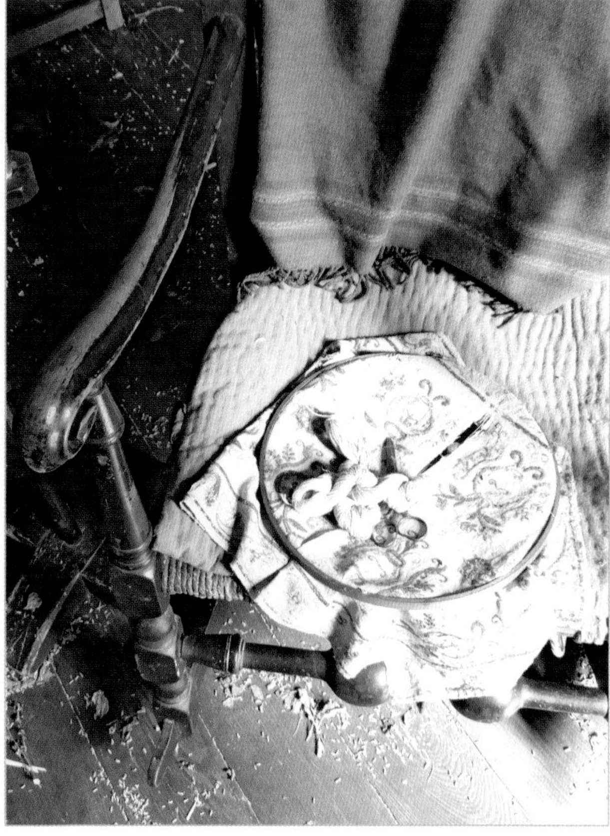

This corner conversation area of the sitting room is pleasantly inviting. The owner has good taste in furniture placement and textile choice. All eyes are attracted to the sofa; it has well chosen upholstery and its legs allow the eye to continue under it which is a good thing.

Period home enthusiasts agree we do need electricity but authenticators also want their rooms to be as believable as possible to the pre-electricity era. So the best we can accomplish is to diminish an electrical lamp's importance. To do that, we can be choosy where the lamp is placed. We can purchase plain serviceable shades of parchment, tin or copper rather than decorative ones which remind the brain that Mr. Electricity is in the room.

A veteran authenticator strives to diminish, disguise, all outward evidence of electricity from the room as possible, not to enhance it or draw attention to it. Today the era of candle lighting is preferred by a majority of period homeowners. Anytime the 21stC owner can install electrified candle-like lighting devices rather than electrified incandescent bulb lighting with decorative shades, the room will appear more believable.

The fireplace will always be the focal point of any room even if today's homeowner ignores it. It allures people to it. Period homeowners can easily and unknowingly demean a fireplace's importance in two ways. First, furniture can be ill-placed around the fireplace. For example in some photographed period homes, the sofa's backside can be seen facing the fireplace to enable a modern conversation area. Any fireplace would recoil from such an attack on its reputation!

Secondly a fireplace can be demeaned when the homeowner accessorizes it wrongly. If this pictured fireplace is in a keeping room, then it is accessorized correctly. But if the fireplace is in a sitting room or family parlor, it should be staged as a parlor fireplace with no cooking equipment except perhaps a tea kettle.

Fire maintenance tools are important and needed to attend safely to the parlor coals. The mantel would host a candlestick or two, a few books, maybe a chalkware piece, or small framed watercolor or calligraphy.

When a room, a fireplace and its correct accessories come together, the room invokes believability, and that is a tenet of authenticating worth achieving.One goal of an authenticator is to remove incongruities from a room. This is important because unrelated objects in the room put into question the room's purpose. We can imagine the mind talking to itself saying "Oh My! This is a family parlor but now I'm not so sure because there are kitchen items in this room." Successful period rooms are those that we enter and see the room's purpose quickly and clearly and then later leave the room impressed with no doubt ever in our mind of the room's purpose. Incongruities weaken a period room's purpose more than most homeowners would believe.

In this photo above, the eye could be confused due to the upper class elements of an oil portrait, pewter chandelier, the extra full yardage curtains and the turret ceiling. These stand in contrast to the working class objects: the make-do chair, the primitive desk, cupboard, settle, barn lantern and spinning equipage. A veteran authenticator would see these incongruities but also as easy corrections.

This subject is discussed here because some period homeowners know their room needs improvement but they know not the problem. Often the solution is simple – eliminate the incongruities.

This attractive and colorful room holds an important example for authenticators to consider which is the change of curtain styles within the period home. Certainly it would be an easier choice to select one curtain style and install it throughout several rooms but it is not what the early housewife would have done. The best fabric afforded with the most current fashionable curtain style was installed in the public parlor or sitting room. Other rooms had less valuable fabric and less genteel styled window coverings.

This pleasant room has a simple one panel curtain but is draped in a manner that brings both softness and formality to the room. But what if this same draped curtain appeared in every public room of the house – the parlor/sitting room, the guest bedroom, the dining room? Would it not be boring? True the housewife of the past may have had only one fabric with which to hand sew all her curtains but she would have tied some curtains for the lesser rooms, draped others for the family's sitting room, pulled back those in the parlor and shuttered the bedroom windows.

Each adaptation gave a totally different appearance to her one fabric use curtains. To the authenticator, it is important that the curtain style meets the character of the three types of rooms within their dwellings – the work room (no window coverings), the family rooms (a basic curtain that fits the family's needs), the public room (a fancier window covering than in the family space). In the past, window coverings announced to the visitor the economic status of the 18th and early 19thC household. The serious authenticator will do the same today.

Purchasing signage for interior display is popular among some country and period style home enthusiasts. It's a fun purchase as seen by this sign "Apples for sale". But for the veteran authenticator, signage is seldom wanted interiorly. If signage is purchased, we would bet the signage will be used for one reason only – the buyer has a taproom in his restored tavern and he needs to announce prices of comestibles and liquors. In past centuries signboards were vital to all – especially stage coach or horseback travelers; the inn's outdoor signboard informed all road travelers that a night's lodging and drink was available. Rural housewives advertised their cheese, eggs, bread for sale by signboards. Every merchant in town had a prominent shingle over the street. Today signage often exists at the front entrance of a private period house, proclaiming the dwelling's historic construction date and builder or present owners. But signage in an authenticated room is one object that will demean a room's character; the mind sees a signboard in a room as a bold foreigner.

Repeatedly we've talked of objects in a room must speak to the purpose of the room. Here, this decorator has placed a lovely 19thC corner cupboard in original paint in this sitting room but has used the shelves to display objects which do not belong in the sitting room but rather the work room.

Here are some suggestions of how this sitting Room cupboard could be 'dressed'.

Old books could fill an entire shelf but they bring some demands with them. They do not want to be placed by graduated size. So authenticators be alert when placing books on a cupboard shelf. Do place the best looking and oldest ones in the center of the shelf as the eye will go to the center first. The oldest bound books have horizontal ridges on the spine so be sure they are placed center. Books should not be staged as a nice view but as if the books have been read and replaced. Finally, in every book put a bay leaf or two for insect control. Books should be on a shelf easily reached for reading.

Document boxes could occupy one shelf. These can be tin, wood or leather and should be various sizes from shoebox size to as large as will fit the shelf. Allow the lid of one of the document boxes to remain open then place some rolled up documents, real or faux, in the box. Roll the fake documents around a cardboard tube and tie with a narrow plain ribbon. You can even seal with red wax. Pen a person's name, date, specify the court and court case number on the outside of the faux document. Place these fake documents in and around the document box. This faux document creation would be a good 'mother and child' activity not only for the value of doing something together but also for the educational value of informing children about landed property, courthouse records and the history of land transfers in your family. Hobby Lobby has all the pen, ink, paper and ribbon supplies needed.

Another shelf could exhibit family historic objects such as silhouettes and small oil portraits which could lean against a shelf's back board. Other objects might include great-great grandmother's marriage slippers, a family diary or copy of Revolutionary War muster papers. These objects can be your own family's historical belongings or purchased ones portrayed as part of your family's history.

This memorabilia was gathered together in a parlor or sitting room in early homes for the purpose of conversation with house guests. During the timeframe of this volume, 1780-1840, there had already been several small Indian Wars and the Revolutionary War was very fresh in the citizen's mind. The War of 1812 had occurred and the struggles of the Civil War were just ahead. With all these military actions over those 60-70 years, most families acquired a trail of artifacts which would have been displayed in a sitting room or parlor cupboard as discussed here.

A parlor like this fine example was afforded by an upper class family, possibly of landed gentry or of a seafaring captain. Today's homeowner has invited history as a partner and it's obvious. The mirror's only purpose was to reflect daylight and candlelight in an 18thC dwelling. Its wall position was carefully selected for the best reflection which added a bright spot to the room. The porcelain Chinese ginger jars were exported from China to America filled with ginger, a rare spice in its day. In America these jars also stored oil, herbs and salt. Artwork and oil portraits were expected in fine parlors. The young lady in this frame is attired with a neckpiece called a ruff. It is made of handmade bobbin lace or of lawn fabric. Ruffs were worn among the wealthy and the royals in the 16thC by both women and men. Brass candlesticks anchor the mantel. But note, today's homeowner could have displayed several ginger jars and several candlesticks on the mantel but discipline ruled instead, thank goodness. The silver tea set is complete. Porcelain teacups and linen napkins were carefully chosen but where is the table covering? From America's colonial days, the genteel families covered their tea table with the family's best linen, even when not in use. If improvements were wanted in this fine parlor, the tablecloth must be present and the easy chairs fitted with wool or linen.

In past centuries and until WW I, the rural housewife saved space in her sitting room, sometimes in a large kitchen, for a narrow daybed or cot. It was a nearby napping place for a child or for the farmer who needed a quick shut-eye after a big noon meal.

This bed discloses more truth than just being a resting place for a hard working farmer. It reveals the family's work habits, the family's middle class status and its pride of achievement but not so proud that would prevent a bed in their best public room.

Sometimes a piece of furniture appears to be out of place in a period room such as this daybed but maybe it's not out of place for the social class that dwells within. The economic status affixed to the different occupations of the 18th and 19th centuries determined how a family fitted out their rooms.

Serious authenticators might reconsider how a room is affected by social and economical issues. Certainly a farm family lived differently than an urban family did, even when the income earned was equivalent. The farm's needs always ruled. Without a healthy farm, there was no livelihood for the rural family.

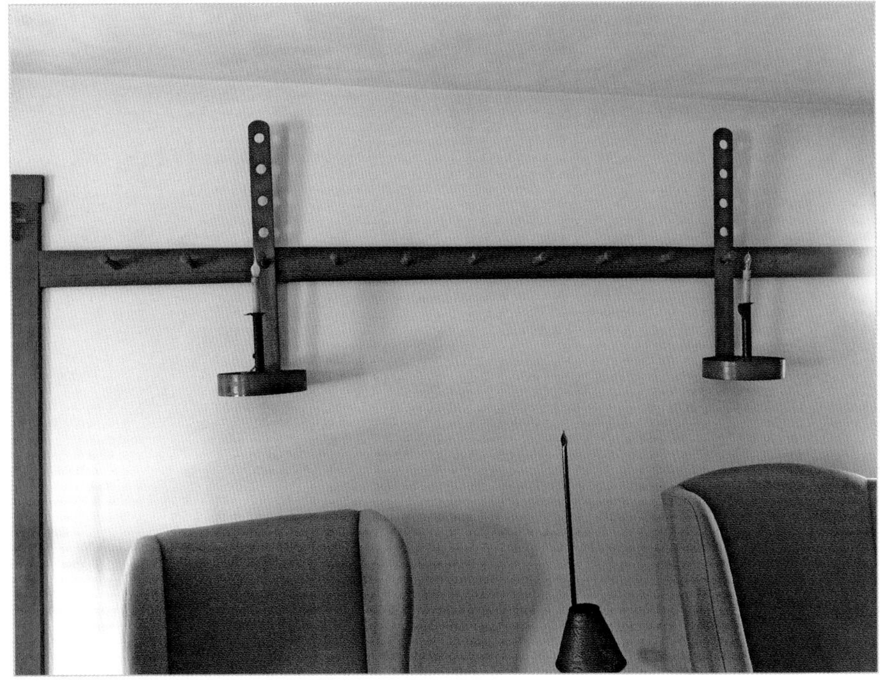

Pegboard, also called a peg rail, is a common wall element in period homes today. The Shakers were well known for their rooms of useful pegboard on which the Shakers hung ladderback chairs, small footstools, lengths of fabric to shield cold walls, small household tools and their famous wood candle sconces.

The Shakers installed pegboards between windows, or from a doorframe to a window's woodwork or room corner. The Shakers commonly installed pegboards completely around the entire room. It was never positioned on a wall without beginning or ending with some vertical woodwork. This implementation was necessary because the pegboard was installed before plaster was applied. Thus the pegboard's face appeared nearly flush with the plaster.

Pegrails very often appear badly in country and period homes because they are nailed into the wall without regard of any beginning or ending points. The worst scenario is the same lonely pegrail in the middle of a wall AND loaded with objects that relate in no way to that room.

The secretary bookcase fit the needs of early Virginia movers after settling in the Ohio Country. Their migration had been lightly outfitted and their log domicile small but eventually furniture could be afforded. One furniture piece with two purposes fits their lifestyle. This secretary bookcase did double duty – serving as a bookcase and a writing/reading surface. Letters from Virginia were kept here and read over and over. Accounts were recorded. Books brought from Frederick County were safely stored here with tansy interspersed among them. Ink, paper, legal documents and the cherished land warrant set accessible on the bottom shelf. The flat surface of the secretary served to teach children their numbers, evening Bible reading took place here, often with a tanned deer hide on its writing surface. The wall received any nailed sale bills, notes to be paid, a reminder when the cow freshened and maybe a framed family record. In its day, this secretary bookcase needed only a chair. No extra accessories are needed when an authenticator portrays this piece of furniture honestly.

It is uncertain whether this corner cupboard is in a dining room or parlor but it is indeed handsome and is enhanced by the pewter. In fact, its character is obvious enough that it needs no gravy-train riders; the objects on its top seem unimportant. While the decorator often adds insignificant items to a cupboard, the authenticator would return the coverlet to a bedstead.

Chapter 6

The Keeping Room

The term 'keeping room' originated in New England. It describes a family's living space where the family was maintained and cared for and labored in one room.

Fireplace cooking and family meals were taken here. The family often also slept here.

Visitors were received. Family members were married and died in this room. Daily work was continuously astir – spinning, sewing, mending harness, cutting shoe pegs, bullet making, carding wool.

Sometimes a fireplace is built so handsomely yet it is so boring. Not the case here for the homeowners have made this fireplace talk. By the ash heap, some cooking has taken place and cloth articles are drying high enough to avoid shooting embers.

Herbs are not yet dry enough for storage but husband has provided a new oven closure which replaces a badly worn one.

The Rumford fireplace has all of its necessary equipment, and in addition, it is not burdened with a large collection of fireplace artifacts as some fireplaces are. This is an active cooking hearth hence an iron 'fireback' protects the firebox's back wall so the brick masonry is not damaged by heat.

Bread making was an early lesson for the household's young daughter but bread baking was one of the last lessons trusted to her. Bread, the staff of life, was never put to risk.

When substance fails, create a story line then add the specific objects to make the scene speak.

A camera image is always truthful. Here the general store bin juxtaposed to an upholstered settee disturbs the mindset of a comfortable sitting room beyond when viewed from this camera angle. Indeed the green bin piece is handsome and its owner has correctly added believable products to it, but a rectangular work table or a kitchen chest would lessen the conflict between the sitting room's settee and the kitchen's general store bins. Listen! You can hear these two pieces bickering. The settee wants this social climber off its back and the general store bin is eager to join the pantry where it can dominate.

A digital photo will alert a homeowner to faults in a room even before the human eye recognizes them as faults.

Both indoor and outdoor signboards are very popular among country decorators but authenticators must be more discerning. Use of signage inside a contemporary 18th or early 19thC household was indeed rare. No hair-plastered or wood plank wall needed a directive or authorization from a signboard! However if the dwelling had a public taproom within its domain, staged with tavern tables and caged bar, then a posting of liquors and prices on a signboard were visible and today's authenticator would want to duplicate that scene.

In the 1700s and 1800s outdoor signage was a benefit and an advertisement for any hostelry, stage inn, tavern stand, mill site or land office. A painted placard or flat board was attached onto a building's exterior or on a wayside post with name, date and an iconic image. This signboard was expected and recognizable by locals and travelers alike who could or could not read!

Signage in an authenticated room will demean the period room but signage outdoors will rightly add significance to a period property. Signage becomes faulty when it is displayed in the wrong place; it becomes meaningful when the sign's message relates to a nearby structure.

Here is the low table that stands before the fireplace with the cushioned ladderback chair in view. This table with a blue painted base has one candle which seems inadequate today but it was common before the Civil War for a family to gather around one candle in an evening. Many 18th and early 19thC travel journals and women's diaries document this home activity. One candle lit the darkness for a family's evening of reading, handiwork and discussions of next day's chores. Decorators display lots of candles in their homes because candles visually represent the past. However the authenticator knows candles were a laborious necessity for the rural household and were an expensive purchase for the urban dweller. Neither of the rural or urban middle class households would have used two candleholders in one room. Sometimes for fun, hold family talks around one candle and teach the grandchildren about candlepower, candleberry, candlewood, and the measured unit of footcandle

A long table conjures in our mind the gathering of a large family for a wholesome meal. It is the magnet of the American family. Six old bentwood chairs add more nostalgia for a sit-down meal. This modern day homeowner, wishes to appreciate the beautiful patina of the plank top boards, and rightly so.

The American housewife had the table covered with cloth whether the table was in use or not. This notion came to America even with the Plimoth pilgrims in the 1600s. From then the American dinner table was covered until the 1950-60s. Only the poorest family ate on a bare wood surface. If the meal table also served as a work table, the table covering or tablecloth was folded back onto the table end while the pie crust was rolled.

When an authenticator can envision the workings of a period kitchen, better decisions will be made about its interior. Envision it then believe it, then install believable accessories.

Simplicity always allows a room's strengths to manifest. This dining room's strengths are easily seen here. The stenciled wall motif attracts the eye upward which is a good thing. Amateur decorators usually overlook the importance of upward eye travel then wonder why their room lacks character. This homeowner already knows this lesson. The six arm chandelier would not have been afforded by a middle class family. Chandeliers were installed in this era in public buildings at tax payer expense. When a good meal and pewter join forces, a dining room needs little else. So the homeowner choice of understated curtains is good.

Here is another lesson this room offers. Pewter placed as a table centerpiece and a "ready to serve" pewter tea/coffee service on the side table are both attractive and relative but maybe a little static. What if the pewter candlesticks and charger on the table were set on a white linen table covering with cheese and coffee added with the fruit? Now the scene speaks and seemingly awaits the arrival of the first partaker.

If any improvement were wanted in this view, the Albany slip pitchers could be removed to the kitchen. They demean the room's pewter, formerly known as the poor man's silver.

A mustard dresser is a great choice for a dining room; it is fitted out with redware.

An authenticator would be quite choosy as to which pieces of redware should remain as dresser contents. Authenticators enjoy displaying redware as the early housewife would have placed it. They know there was redware that was for the dinner table and redware pieces that prepared and stored food; these belonged in a kitchen or pantry.

Surely the reader will agree that this dining room is well appointed, has a relaxing atmosphere and is a good example of a country decorated dining room. But what if in the years ahead the owners ask 'How would the 1820s "goodwife" have furnished this room?'

Let's walk through this room. In the foreground is an uncovered table. Today's runner would not be present in 1820s but a linen table covering would be. A chandelier was only found in heavily tithed churches, courtrooms, and land offices but installed here is a wall sconce and candled devices on the mantel which would have served the room well enough in 1820. There are topiaries on the mantel; the middling goodwife probably never saw such a thing. The crockery on top of the cupboard was in their day solely utilitarian, belonging in the kitchen, pantry or work room and in that space was filled with larded meat, kraut or baked cookies. Ancestral oil portraits are wall hung as they were in 1820s in some upper middle class homes. Stenciling during its heyday (1790 to 1840) was cheaper than wallpapering a wall so it was an attractive alternative for the upper middle class. Crockery has a talent for sneaking into a room. How they accomplish this no one knows.

The corner fireplace is instant atmosphere. Its paint color is restful for the eye.

The idea of a separate dining room was a space only afforded by the affluent class in early America. It was a sensational event when Thomas Jefferson built one at Monticello. By 1850s, the middle class Germans were still partaking their meals at small tables wherever convenient in the house.

For the authenticator who portrays the 18th or early 19thC middle class household, here are some points to recreate the middle class eating experience. Instead of one long harvest table, use a couple smaller tables in one room.

Your middle class ancestors dined this way until the Gay 1890s. Before 1890s the kitchen work table became the meal table for four to six persons. If the size of your ancestor's family required another table, it was found in the family parlor or sitting room next to the kitchen.

This room is where the decorator needs discipline as more often than not the inclination is to accessorize this room with bowls, barrels, crockery, redware, yellow ware or pantry boxes, to name but a few choices. As seen in each picture, this homeowner has not fallen to that temptation.

The authenticator will keep the family parlor as a family parlor and the kitchen as a kitchen.

Once kitchen related items sneak into this adapted eating space, the authenticator has destroyed the adventure of a well-done interior. An authenticated space is always ruined when purposeful items belonging to one room spill over into another purposeful room. The eye loves its adventure from room to room but when the eye recognizes wooden bowls in every room, crockery in every room and work baskets in every room, the mind records this as "same-o, same-o sameness" and adventure is lost. The eye and the mind then make a run for an escape from the house.

The space in which a family "took meals" indicated the economic status of that family. From colonial days onward, the affluent household dined in a formal room while the middle class partook their meals in a kitchen or keeping room. The poor ate food wherever convenience could be found, usually without a table or chair. Within the stratum of the middle class, meals were eaten at various tables in the house. Children ate standing at the meal table or at the kitchen dresser while parents and older working children sat at the table. Some family members "took their meal", literally carried, their meal to a bedchamber.

Here in this view two family members are about to partake of shared food. The meal could be in a middle class back parlor, a kitchen, or a bedchamber. However the candle would not be lit until eventide to save tallow.

A keeping room was a multi-purpose room characteristic of the earliest American dwellings. It was the largest room of a house, sometimes the largest and only room. Not only was the room itself of multiple uses but so also were the furnishings. A table was the meal table, a work top, an ironing board or a butchering surface. A banc-lit was a bench and a pull-out bed. A settle could be a chair and table.

Many work scenes are noticed here – cooking food, preserving foodstuffs, preparing herbal remedies, roasting meats, linen cloths have been woven, pewter has been scoured and gourds have been cured. The keeping room was a busy place but also a place of family entertainment such as evening singing, reading, knitting and visits from neighbors. It was also a place of rest as a bedstead was very often in this room. Here also was the smaller daybed used as a sick bed when needed. And for family protection, the flintlock was kept not above the mantel but hung over the entrance door or laid on a joist beam.

In the keeping room, all the needs of the family were met and kept.

One of the tenets of the authenticating process is "to enhance the positives in the room and to remove the negatives". But sometimes a wonderful positive element acquires a negative element and that is a harmful thing. Here is an eye-catching positive – the ceiling with old thick joists. Sadly, they have been distressed with a tool that leaves modern marks. How believable they would be had they been distressed with the blade of an adze instead of a modern chisel or hatchet.

Notice the pegged beam and yes . . . that is a mouse!

This homeowner has established an attractive country style dining room that would please all country style decorators. We can praise the owner for the handsome table and choice of reproduced bow back painted chairs. The painted cupboards are useful and add color to the room. The upper walls have a wide wallpaper border which attracts the eye up which is important in any interior. This housekeeper has done some homework knowing how a sugar cone should be displayed and is a keen collector of woodenware. The room is a successful country decorated dining room.

Now let's discuss how the room would be changed by an authenticator. First, all items that perform work would be removed from the dining room to a work place in or near the home such as the kitchen, the pantry, a rear work room or the dooryard outside the back entry. Here are those items: the hominy mortar, the candle tree, the butter churns, the dough box, the gourds and pumpkins, the primitive bench, the wooden bowls, the breadboard, the market basket, and trestle table. Here's a test. Be an authenticator and place these objects where you think they belong. Hint: two items should be in the dooryard.

The table's centerpiece is another change that an authenticator would make. The hominy mortar and gourds would be removed The sugar cone remains but needs sugar nippers for a diner's benefit. Likewise the sugar cone should be unwrapped of its cheesecloth for this dining room appearance. If the sugar cone is being stored in a kitchen, it would be wrapped in cheesecloth for fly protection. Added to the dining table's center could be a glass covered salt cellar, a glass vinegar cruet and a bowl of farm fruits. When all objects in a room relate to the purpose of the room, the room gains conformity which strengthens the room's importance.

Chapter 7

The Taproom and Tavern Room

Tavern keeping was a good fit for a widow and her children but it was laborious. With a couple of strong sons, daughters that could cook, and a spare room or two, the family dwelling could be a successful tavern stand which is the period term for a tavern site, if located on a well-traveled road. This Ohio authenticator here has successfully portrayed this scenario.

Here is the taproom where locals and travelers could discuss news and rumors, down some liquid fortification, get warm in winter by the fireside and maybe do some trading. The room's smoky walls and all the broken pipes on the floor are evidence of the copious use of tobacco among men and women, and yes, even women smoked pipes. Table games, betting, spitting competitions and spilled ale were common within the taproom.

Many period home publications today often erroneously use the term "tavern room" for "taproom". An early tavern was a licensed place, an inn, public house or stagecoach stand, where liquor was stored and often where hospitality and entertainment could be obtained. A taproom was a room in a tavern in which liquor was sold from a bar to be drunk on the premises.

Giving voice to correct terminology of the past automatically directs the authenticator's mindset into another era. Use the old terms and enjoy your journey into the 18th or early 19th centuries.

Seldom was a tavern's taproom quiet and peaceful under the influence of "drink" in our timeframe of the 18th and early 19th centuries. From this photo view, some rowdiness has occurred – a tipped over ladderback, a beer mug emptied over the table and onto the floor. No wonder the wet floor puddle has given the place an aroma of yeasty beer. What fun it is to be an authenticator!

Not every taproom had a caged bar but for a widowed tavern owner who must keep her eye on the many activities of the tavern stand, it was a great convenience and worth its expense constructing it. While imbibers were yet in the taproom, a busy tavern keeper did cage the bar by lowering and locking the overhead "wicket". No taverner could then pour or steal any contents of the bar. A caged bar's wicket is a series of balusters within a wooden frame which can be raised, rope tied or hooked to the ceiling to open the bar or lowered to close and secure it.

Sometimes musicians of the road stopped for the night and bartered their talents for a night's sleep on a straw pallet. Prospects of evening entertainment spread quickly in the settlement and soon the locals filled the tavern; skins could be bought and sold, garments could be won or lost in cards. On a drinker's greatcoat, now known as a heavy overcoat, a dog sleeps. The tavern owner posts a broadsheet, now called a broadside, setting new liquor prices.

These above activities could all be exemplary scenes staged by any authenticator owning a taproom. Incorporate them and enjoy your very believable taproom.

The rural tavern keeper had to supply food for road travelers. This was a requirement of licensing plus the local authorities set the price of the liquors sold. This taproom has several meal tables. The bar is provisioned with ale, beer, and whiskey but also foodstuffs such as corned beef, venison jerky and always rounds of bread and cheese were available for a price. For locals who could read, checking the sale bills and the "lost and found" notices nailed to the taproom walls was beneficial. Evidence of simple food, sale bills, public announcements should be noticeable in a well-staged taproom.

Many lessons can be learned from this well executed taproom. One is that a taproom is far more than a space for comestibles and drink. It was also a community meeting place and that should be very obvious in the staging.

When the authenticator knows the true purpose of a period room and how the early family worked and lived in that space, then that authenticator is headed down an exciting path.

But there is always more reading, research ahead and don't forget to 'conjure up a pretend period family' to aid you along the way.

Sherry and I must reiterate the intent *of Authenticating a Country Dwelling* as a learning experience. Hopefully you have now gained an appreciation of what the rooms of an authentic 18th or 19thC period home would look like and could discern the difference between it and a country decorated home. I suspect you have also realized that the 'authenticator' is someone who not only possesses a knowledge of and interest in history, but who also has an active imagination! The message we hope you the reader has gleaned from having read the book is that we, both the decorator and the authenticator, have a creative heart and it is only the difference in mind-set between the two which sets the course of what appearance a room will take. I believe we kindred spirits have an intuitive talent and more than likely, without too much effort, could each conjure up our own 'pretend family' to guide us in authenticating our homes should we choose to do so.

Upon leaving the home of one authenticator whose home I had just photographed for the book, I commented that it was obvious how much this homeowner loved life. She responded that her 'imagined life' not only added a dimension to everyday living but an outlet for her creative talents and a structure for what she placed in her home and the overall 'feeling' she was trying to achieve.

Sherry and I wish to give special thanks to the many homeowners who allowed us the use of their homes as a tool to demonstrate an educational concept not to mention their trust in working with us on this venture and first-ever book of this type. In no way was our intent at any time to criticize or critique any homeowner's style of décor or talents. Further, we acknowledge that not everyone chooses to be an authenticator and live in a setting which requires some sacrifices of our modern day conveniences. We appreciate that many of us are not only content with the awesome homes we've created but are proud of that accomplishment and rightly so.

Authenticating a Country Dwelling would not have been possible without the permission of the following participants in no special order:

Bill and Pam Bausmith, Bud and Louise Villa, John and Joy Henson, Pat Linton, Lily Hall, Michael and Barbara Burnett, Les and Sharon Blanton, Daniel and Anita McCann, Lowell and Wanda Burton, Carolyn Carter, Helen Brown, George and Sandra Wilder, Mike Spangler, Arthur and Beth Russo, Steve and Leslie Powell, Rich and Melanie Lortie, Marjorie Staufer, Bob and Criss Cefus, Keith and Jo Corbett, Ray and Geri Taylor, Art and Vicki Martin, David Kay and Nancy Bryer, Paul and Robin Miller, Dave and Debbie Mansfield, Chuck and Marion Atten, Mike and Angie Ditmer and finally Craig and Gay Schneeman.

Sherry and I wish you much success in *Authenticating a Country Dwelling*!